Death in the Delta

Death in the Delta

Uncovering a Mississippi Family Secret

❧

Molly Walling

University Press of Mississippi / *Jackson*

Willie Morris Books in Memoir and Biography

www.upress.state.ms.us

The University Press of Mississippi is a member
of the Association of American University Presses.

Disclaimer about Some Characters
The true story that appears in these pages has been
written to the best of my recollection. Some few
characters, however, are composites. Others have
fictitious names and/or altered identifying
characteristics so as to protect their anonymity.

First printing 2012

∞

Library of Congress Cataloging-in-Publication Data

Walling, Molly.
Death in the delta : uncovering a Mississippi family
secret / Molly Walling.
pages cm. — (Willie Morris books in memoir and
biography)
ISBN 978-1-61703-609-5 (cloth : alk. paper) —
ISBN 978-1-61703-610-1 (ebook) 1. Anguilla
(Miss.)—Race relations. 2. Gunfights—Mississippi—
Anguilla—History—20th century. 3. Manslaughter—
Mississippi—Anguilla—History—20th century.
4. Family secrets—Mississippi—Anguilla—
Case studies. 5. Fields, Harris Jesse, 1922–2000.
6. Walling, Molly—Family. I. Title.
F349.A54W35 2012
305.8009762'414—dc23   2012005302

British Library Cataloging-in-Publication Data available

for Jay
and for Grace, Jack, and Maddie

To strive, to seek, to find, and not to yield.

—ALFRED, LORD TENNYSON, *Ulysses*

Contents

Primary Players

Narrator: Molly Walling

The Fields Family in Anguilla, Mississippi
Jesse Rawles Fields (moved to Anguilla, 1842)
    Harris Jesse Fields + Martha Katherine Sullivan
        (thirteen children)
        Thomas Walter Fields + Rebekah (Mamaw, Miss Beck)
            Harris Jesse (Big Jay) + Betsy Fleming
                Jay
                Molly
                Laura
            Tom Fields
            Bill Fields
            Sis Fields

12 December 1946, Shoot-Out at the Pan Am Station
    David Jones
    Simon Toombs
        Rose Cooper (Simon's niece)
            Emma Harris (Rose's daughter)
        Inez Files (Simon's niece)

Secondary Players
(In Order of Appearance)

Aunt Mat and Jo(sephine)	Servants at Greenfields (Fields home)
Mary and Joe Fleming	Betsy's parents/Big Jay's in-laws

Joseph Henry Fleming III	Betsy's brother
Hodding Carter	Editor, Greenville *Delta Democrat Times*
Sheriff Crawford	Sharkey County sheriff— arrested Dad
Hugh and Mary Dayle McCormick	McCormick Book Inn—Greenville
Trudy Shultz m.	Mary Dayle's mother and Betsy's friend
Jack Shultz	Photographer—*Deer Creek Pilot*
Ray Mosby	Current editor—*Deer Creek Pilot*
Pat Thrasher	Deputy clerk—Sharkey County Courthouse
Merlin Richardson	Mayor of Anguilla
King Evans	Ninety-three-year-old witness
Carolyn Hackett	King's daughter
Dr. Goodman	Pronounced men dead/ treated Tom
Carabelle Johnson	Dr. Goodman's black nurse
Cunninghams (daughter Lynn)	Bristol neighbors
Goodpastures (daughter Lean, son Frank)	Bristol neighbors
Kramers (Bill and Katie, son Josh)	Bristol neighbors
Charles Weissinger	Anguilla attorney
Fielding Wright	Lieutenant and acting governor— Mississippi
Elbert Hilliard	Retired archivist
"Gip"	Mamaw's gin manager
Jo Anderson	Gip's daughter

Prologue

Two stories are imbedded in this narrative. The first tale is a deeply held, sixty-year family secret that came to light in 2006, and involved the murder of two black men in the Mississippi Delta after World War II. The perpetrator was, allegedly, my father. At first, I was confused and overwhelmed by the weightiness of the event. My only recourse was to take in the family version of the story and pursue a larger truth, one that would reveal hidden causes and consequences. All of the men directly involved, black and white, were dead. My aunts and close family friends warned, cajoled, and begged me not to dig, but rather to "let sleeping dogs lie." I couldn't follow their wishes. Instead I trekked on, picking up crumbs of memory along a narrow trail. At first, I heard so many vivid renditions of the story that I started looking under rocks for sources outside the scope of the drama. There was no paper trail, as you will see, except for newspaper accounts. I interviewed and tape-recorded descendents of the principals involved as well as a ninety-three-year-old witness. I consulted newspaper accounts, deed books, and other records.

Embedded in the discoveries of my truth-seeking story are memories of another time, one that depicts the gradual collapse of a way of life. Taken together, the two narratives create a detailed portrait of an important moment in our collective American history, a moment that can inform us all.

I have crafted this narrative by bringing in bits and pieces of various accounts to reveal a whole picture. Nuances of language, its syntax and structure, came from recorded conversations, as did the attitudes and beliefs reflected there. I read historical accounts of the 1940s and 1950s to find context and perspective. I wandered deep into my family's history and deep into the complex racial dynamics at play in southern life before the Civil

Rights Movement. I listened to many voices. Truth-telling, no matter from whose perspective, is often painful though ultimately liberating. In the end, our stories reveal both the darkness and the beautiful light of our human nature.

I am acutely aware of the hard work the people of Mississippi have undertaken for years to overcome the past and step into an era of racial equality. Today there exists a new culture very different from the one that prevailed in the 1940s. Hodding Carter III told me that my story is one "most white Mississippians prefer to bury, but so do most people everywhere." As Ray Mosby, current editor of the Sharkey County bimonthly newspaper, the *Deer Creek Pilot*, so eloquently put it, "Mississippi is going through this soul searching, gut-wrenching experience of trying to make up for previous ills. There are enough [grievous stories] known without looking for another one to cauterize." Let me be clear. It is not my intention to reinjure or denigrate anyone, but rather to tell you my story.

Death in the Delta

CHAPTER ONE

Out of the Blue

March 2006

The phone rang. It was my brother, Jay, calling from the road, driving from our uncle Tom's funeral in the Florida Panhandle home to Asheville. He had something startling to tell me. It could have been anything, if it had to do with our family—some oddity, strangeness, eccentricity.

"Hey. How was the funeral? Who did you see?"

He bypassed the usual "catch me up on the family" details and plunged headfirst into the thing that was on his mind. "Molly, you're not gonna believe what I heard about Dad."

"What?" The mere mention of my father sent the muscles in my stomach into spasm even though six years had passed since we buried him. Jay began by telling me that Uncle Tom's son, our cousin, drew him aside and asked if he knew about the "shoot-out" in Anguilla (Mississippi, our ancestral home).

"Tommy told me Uncle Tom had a scar on his shoulder. He'd always assumed that it was from a battle wound he'd suffered during combat in the Pacific Theatre. But before he died, Unc told him it came from a shoot-out in the Delta. Seems Dad and Tom went lookin' for a black field hand who stole a car—either from the plantation or the gin. They followed him to a honky-tonk and a fight broke out. The man pulled a gun. Dad shot him, and Tom was injured somehow." Tommy also said that they had followed this worker who drove off in a brand-new company vehicle to pick up a piece of machinery. He didn't return the car but went, instead, to the dive to get drunk. When Dad or Tom found him and asked for the keys to the car, he refused and pulled a gun that he fired at Uncle Tom. Then Dad reached for his own gun and shot the man dead.

"Dad . . . shot a man?"

"Yeah . . . killed him."

Immediately I started pacing back and forth between the den and kitchen, rubbing my forehead as if to clear my mind so that this news could come in. Jay picked up the conversation, sharing other family news that was more mundane in nature. But I wasn't listening to him.

I couldn't believe what he had told me. It rattled around in my brain for the next couple of days, challenging long-held beliefs that I had tried to tell myself about my father. I felt deeply confused, didn't sleep, couldn't think about anything else. Though I trusted Uncle Tom to get things right, I wasn't sure I could believe this story. Why was Dad there? Who did he shoot? What provoked it? I caught myself standing still, shaking my head. This dreadful event had to have happened in the mid-'40s when Mom and Dad were newly married and living near my grandmother Fields on the family plantation in the Mississippi Delta.

At just about any other time in my life, I would have filed this story away, so caught up was I in getting an education, raising a family of my own, starting careers, but my life had taken on a new rhythm, timbre, and set of lyrics. Marching in place for the first time in many years, I was open to discovery, to taking in stories and inhabiting them. How did I get to this place? A major change in my marital status had occurred five years before Jay's phone call.

Fall 2001, Asheville, North Carolina

One week before the September 11 attack on New York City, I moved to Asheville. I sat on the floor of my bungalow, surrounded by boxes, and watched the planes fly into the towers. That morning, the fresh start I was making with my life seemed even more precarious, though I had my family all around me in those boxes. Photographs, genealogy charts, letters, my father's baby book, my mother's wedding portrait, taped conversations with relatives about family history. The comfort of perpetuity was just about all I had.

Why did I choose Asheville? Even though it had been two years since the split along the fault line in my thirty-year marriage, the terrain I had traversed every day in my hometown of Bristol, Virginia, had become an emotional Siberia. Our broken relationship affected everyone we knew. The damage traveled out in concentric circles so that more and more I had to step cautiously to avoid the pain.

I believe in a merciful God. No other force could have set me free from the life I had lived for so long. But after my divorce, when I took an inventory of my life: no husband, an empty nest, no occupational future, scarce single women friends, I determined that the only antidote would be to move. I spent hours studying the deluxe edition of the *Rand McNally Road Atlas* trying to find a geographic cure, and there was only one place in America that had any appeal. I knew only two people living on the other side of the Blue Ridge Mountains, less than two hours away in Asheville: my Jungian analyst and my brother, Jay. A tiny thread of hope for a better life. I resigned my post as adjunct English teacher at the community college in Abingdon, Virginia. I cancelled the meditation and yoga classes I had begun to teach in a mostly blue-collar, conservative, and provincial community. I said good-bye to the dear and loyal friends who had tried their best to keep me in place; I packed up and drove my loaded Volkswagen toward the mountains. Shortly after I crested the ridge at Sam's Gap on Highway 19/23, I could see Mt. Pisgah standing in the distance. A cloud of thick, heavy, and wet darkness hovered over me and then moved north.

March 2006

Five years passed. During that time, I bought an expensive, Swiss-made sewing machine and started piecing together bright and colorful cotton remnants. The exacting mathematics of quilting, the curative effect of working with my hands, the juice of creativity helped to plant my feet on the ground in a city whose natural beauty fosters the lively and unique work of many fine craftsmen and artists. Like my quilts, my life started to come together. I had a new network of friends, a new parish family, and a part-time job teaching writing at a small local college. During that period of adjustment, my need to figure out the enigma that was my father compelled me to write about him. I believed that setting down my thoughts and experiences on paper would help to puzzle out the truth. Two writing courses in the Great Smokies Writing Program provided the will, inspiration, and some of the tools I needed.

When March 2006 came around and my father's brother, Tom Fields, died, I made a hard decision not to go to Florida for his funeral. We had corresponded about various family happenings via e-mail shortly before he succumbed to pulmonary disease and an aortic aneurism. Tom had faced his addiction to alcohol as a young man, and he turned to God with ardent faith that stayed with him until his last day. He was pragmatic and reasonable. I thought that missing his funeral would not be a big deal for him. He was gone. I knew him to be outspoken about his faith, politics, the plight of our poor, our elders, our overgrown government, and he always expressed his thoughts with great humor. I did not know that his death would open up a black hole in our family's history.

A Secret Will Out

I asked myself, "Who was my father?" if what they tell me now is true.

July 18, 1943, North Africa, World War II

From Dad, age twenty, to the family in Anguilla, Mississippi:

Dearest Family,

How my thoughts turn to home and loved ones this beautiful Sunday morning. It's now 20 minutes to 10 and I can see you all bustling around getting dressed for church. "Aunt Mat" is probably rushing around the kitchen, clearing breakfast dishes off the glass top table on the side porch, and fuming because she's going to be late again for church. Bub and Bill are probably in the car and Sis will be reading the funnies. I guess mama will be preparing her Sunday school lesson by now and putting the finishing touches to her hair. "Tater" is probably shining by now in a new suit, with suspenders and an enormous hat with a feather in it. John will have come and gone. Frances is probably entertaining the preacher today.

At the church, the music will start soon and then the men and boys who are finishing last puffs on their cigarettes will file in self-consciously and congregate on the back rows. Aunt Laura will be there and Pa-Paw. Aunt Hal and Uncle Fred, Aunt Rube, Aunt Lil, Burr and Lucille and the boys, Fred Jr. and Dot, Frank and Rufus . . . and all the others will be there—whispering the latest gossip back and forth. Lord, I'd love to be there. I'd love to be able to take a bath in a tub with all the soap and water I wanted to use and put on a clean uniform that Frances had washed and ironed instead of my own sloppy laundering without pressing. I'd like to sit there in the cool and listen to the music and look around me at folks I've known all my life.

On this side of the ocean we're observing the Sabbath in a different way. We've had our church earlier in the little French chapel here. The Catholics met earlier this morning; the Protestants at 8:30, and now the Jewish boys are having their worship services. The chapel is plain and simple. A long narrow building whose only claim of superiority over the other buildings is twice the number of windows, whitewashed walls and a number of hard rough benches. But it's a chapel. It has a cross on top and even though we use it during the week days for school it has a certain air of solemn dignity that makes us wish we had maybe stretched ourselves to the extent of breaking out a clean uniform and shaving before we came in.

During the week we are taught how a certain enemy airplane has no protection overhead, how to employ our guns and bombs so as to take as many lives as many ways as we can. How to shoot a paratrooper, how to kill a sentry with a knife so he can give no alarm of our approach. How we can live off the land if we are forced down in the water.

But this place is still a chapel. When one enters it still feels one degree closer to God. And we love that chapel as much as we love our little churches at home.

Overhead classmates and friends of mine are droning over and away in airplanes. There are low scattered clouds this morning and they peel off on them, zooming through and around them. That's a "rat race," a pilot's biggest sport. I was up earlier and I thought what a fitting preparation for church this is. To float around God's heavens on wings He has given us sense enough to build. To climb and dive and

swoop and zoom around with your temples throbbing, every
nerve awake and aware, your whole being attuned so that you
are a part of the ship, an extra cylinder, an airfoil, and then,
to climax it by a carefully gauged and calibrated approach
to land. "Too fast, too fast, whoa, whoa, slower, slower, now,
flaps down, get that stick forward, okay now, steady, steady
reel it in, nose up, nose up, higher, higher. There you're good,
chop the throttles, hold it, hold it, 'Boom!!'" And you're on
the deck and the landing makes you proud. You climb out
and you're tired, your mind is a vacuum and your nerves and
senses hum like telephone wires. And you drag your weary
self into the chapel and sit and suddenly you are calm, collected and the balm of a voice raised in prayer fills you and
raises you and sets your soul to singing. For a moment you
close your eyes and think, these soiled khakis might be a
Palm Beach suit, and that shoulder touching mine might be
my brother's and this gun on my right hip might be a hym-
nal laid carelessly on my leg and that hunting knife might
be some lady's fan left in the seat. This helmet in my hand
might be a pot of flowers for the altar. Ah but, no, you're still
in Africa with the ocean to cross before you're home but
you don't mind so much. These boys here look like the boys
I went to school with. This landscape out the window might
be Florida but what if it is Africa. You're here among your
own kind with your own place, with your own job to do. You
fit into this crowd. You're an American you're strong you're
smart and you can hold your own with the best of them and
you belong here. So, you see why I'm happy over here. I've
found some place I'm needed, a place I like. A job I can do
'til I drag in my tracks and still enjoy it. But, nowhere I'll ever
go or nothing I'll ever do will take the place of my family and
friends. I love you all and I'm proud of you. I'm proud of my
fine brothers, both bigger than I am now. Bigger but I'll lick
either one of you if you get too big for your britches. My
pretty little Sister—How sweet and lovely you are. My Muz,
how strong, and fine and sweet you are. Maybe someday if

I work hard I'll gain that same strength, that same fineness.
I love you all so much.

There, that about includes everything. All the loves of
my life. My little world. The family, and my airplanes. You
mustn't worry about me. I am getting along better than
I ever have before. I'm well and strong and in the best of
health. I feel good, I am good, and I'm happy. And so I'll
close that way. All my love to you my precious family.
I love you with all my heart.

Jay

Harris Jesse Fields, the man who wrote this letter, was the
father I knew and loved at his best and happiest. Here, at twenty
years old, he expressed those qualities that made him a distinct and gifted man: his love of family, of home, of country; his
pride in the social stratum into which he was born, wealthy and
landed; his faith; his sense of decorum, of personal appearance
and grooming; his love of adventure and the thrill of imminent
danger; and his literate and writerly sensibilities. By the time I
was born, in 1949, his interior world had changed. As his life pro-
gressed, his need to evade the past resulted in a downward spiral.
First he became absorbed in work and later in alcohol. He died in
2000, nearly destitute. There was something about him I couldn't
grasp, and he never let me get close enough to him to figure out
what that was.

After Jay dropped Tommy's family story in my lap, I desperately needed some answers. Finally, I called Dad's sister, Aunt Sis,
in Destin, Florida, to see if she could fill me in, since she was now
the only living sibling in Dad's family.

"Why do you need any details?" she snapped.

"Well, I just don't want to tell it wrong."

"Who needs to hear about it?" Her voice heated up.

Then she opened up.

"It was Thanksgiving and your Mamaw had company coming
from Kentucky. She was in a panic because her housekeeper, Jo,
was out of pocket. Your Mamaw didn't have her 'slave' waiting on

her. Jo was bad about getting drunk and running off to find a man. Your daddy went to find her at a honky-tonk. When he went in, someone turned off the lights. They jumped Jay and Tom. Your dad shot his gun and killed a man. He was in jail but was cleared because it was a case of self-defense. Mamaw covered for them. There was graft involved."

I sat stunned. My mind coursed through the conversation again and again, recalling the subtle nuances of Sis's southern drawl. She was a woman whom I had loved and feared since I was a child. Quick-witted, smart, imposing, she was like my father in the way she barreled into my space, making assumptions and freely expressing her opinions without regard for feelings.

In her speech, Sis didn't filter her own emotions. I knew how she both loved and resented my beloved grandmother. When she said the word "slave" with sarcasm, I sensed she disliked Mamaw's dependence on her hired help, but while Sis was capable of being gracious and loving to the "coloreds" that were fixtures in her family home, her largess was born out of privilege. Same with my dad and his brothers, Tom and Bill, even Mamaw. For them, the advantages of being white, southern, and financially well-off meant that they had power and control over blacks; belittlement and even abuse of them was discretionary.

After the conversation, I found myself slipping back in time, imagining Mamaw's reaction to Jo's untimely disappearance. She would have sought refuge in her bedroom, climbed the two-step riser onto her high canopy bed and heaved her soft, plump body onto the feather mattress. Beneath a crocheted coverlet, dressed only in a slip, silk boxer underwear, and a brassiere with an antique filigreed silver and diamond broach pinned to its mid-section to hold up pendulous breasts, she would have felt the crush of a splitting headache. At that moment, she would have been grateful that all four of her grown children were home safe after the "war to end all wars." How she must have suffered when her boys were away, serving in the military. Dad, the oldest, was heavier than his brothers. He was five feet eleven and weighed about 175 pounds when discharged from the army. Thick, arching eyebrows accented eyes the color of dark coffee, and he had the characteristic proud chin of the Fields clan. He had flown fifty-two missions in a B-17 from Africa to Italy. He had bombed the Axis-held Benedictine fortress-monastery at Monte Cassino and strafed Rommel in the Saharan desert. One of the most important missions he flew was against German oil installations in Ploiesti, Romania, which greatly aided the Allied war effort. Later in his life he told me that his plane, low on fuel, topped the trees during a landing. He walked away in one piece.

Tom, next in line, was a flyboy gunner in the Pacific theatre. And Bill was stationed in the States since the youngest son was not sent out of the country. Aunt Sis was sixteen at that time and a senior in prep school at Stephens College in Missouri.

Mamaw was probably relieved to have her four grown children—alive, well, and safely home with her. But she must have felt she needed the help of her servants, especially at a time like this. From the drawer in her bedside table she would take out a black cloth about the size of a handkerchief and drape it over her face, covering up soft blue eyes. Darkness would have been the only remedy for the dejected mood she was in.

Sis closed our conversation. "Your mother was in Mississippi then. You were a baby. Call her."

Mom and Dad were indeed living in Mississippi then, but I would find out soon enough that Jay was the only baby in the family. At the time, I was just a promise.

CHAPTER THREE

The Scion

Before the heat under a pot of water reaches 212 degrees, the liquid becomes vexed, and it roils around the edges while bubbles rise off the bottom and gain momentum. Mississippi and other southern states began to simmer under new pressures that arose between World War II and *Brown v. Board of Education* in 1954. Even before this pre–civil rights period, the efforts of "rugged individualism" had created a neoplantation system in which each unit was self-contained and ruled at the whim of the owner. In Anguilla, my family at one time owned twenty-five hundred acres and was one of a dozen or so major owners of plantations that size or larger. Productivity was dependent on the labor of blacks who were often descendents of slaves, many of whom moved west from states like Georgia and Alabama. Because blacks who lived on the plantations were either indentured servants or tenant farmers whose living conditions fell far short of the lifestyles of the owners, the two groups had, in effect, parallel lives, only communicating with each other in the confines of the roles they played.

The heat in the Mississippi Delta began to rise when conscripted blacks returned after service in the war. They had experiences unlike anything they could imagine and which did not square up with their established role in Dixie. Some had seen Negro officers who, in rare cases, might have had authority over white soldiers. At the very least, some would have acquired organizational and leadership skills. They had all been issued uniforms and guns and this created a sense of the potential for equal treatment. Upon returning home with new pride, some of these men held their heads a bit higher, dared to be assertive, resisted the domination of their white bosses. They had to have known that parades for returning white soldiers were taking place in cities like Greenville, but there was no such homecoming for them. It didn't take long before the back room at the Pan Am Gas Station in downtown Anguilla began to fill up with African American men, young and old, in pursuit of bootleg alcohol.

My grandmother, widowed at the age of thirty-four in 1935, would have found a headstrong servant to be especially troublesome as she attempted to carry out the responsibilities of financing crops, keeping the cotton gin running, and selling high-quality cotton. Her business acumen had its own learning curve, and she had to have felt pressure knowing that her product had been the leading American export since the early nineteenth century. All of that changed two years after her husband died. Cotton lost its position in the export business and was in oversupply. The Great Depression had driven down the price, and the mechanical cotton picker would soon make weeding and picking cotton a whole new enterprise. These concerns and others made for high anxiety on the plantation.

March 31, 2006

When I thought about Sis's story, I sensed that she was soft-pedaling the events of December 12, 1946. She didn't want me to pursue it, and she expected me to be satisfied that Dad had acted in self-defense. I couldn't fully trust her memory, just like I couldn't fully trust my mother's. Anger and pride, I realized, have a way of subverting the truth, and I would soon learn that each person's story was "a" truth, never "the" truth.

I called my brother, Jay, right away. We were both puzzled and confused. Jay thought it best to approach Sis again himself. He wrote her a lengthy letter and posed some of the questions we shared. He never got an answer.

In the weeks that followed, the sixty-year-old family secret continued to trouble and fascinate me. I was developing an understanding and appreciation for the many facets of Dad's personality, both the good and the dark, but I could not view him as a cold-hearted murderer. At first, I tried to get into his state of mind. I knew his bold, overly responsible, and yet capricious sides. I could see him pulling the trigger without a pause—to defend his brothers and himself. The life he had known from growing up in Mississippi, built on the backs of black men and women, house servants and field hands, was a life he fervently wanted to maintain. Further, Dad, like most white males of that time, didn't place much value on the life of a black man. His arrogance was so great that it overwhelmed any fear of accountability. In many small southern communities like Anguilla, whites projected their own sins onto African Americans who were often held accountable even for unsubstantiated claims.

I wondered why he left home that night with a gun. I could only hope that his plan was to intimidate rather than to kill. At this early stage of discovery, part of me wanted Dad to be deeply remorseful.

ഔ

Another letter that Dad wrote home from North Africa was addressed to Matt and Charley Lee, two of my grandparents' long-standing black workers on the family plantation, called Ashland. Dad wrote:

Matt, I know you and Tater will stay with Mama and look after her the best you can. I don't know what I would do if I didn't know that you older darkies on our place are looking out for everything. I wish it were so that there could be the relationship between the white men and coloured all over the world as it has been with my family and the faithful darkies we have kept for almost a hundred years. Coloured people like yourself, John Parks, Zack Nick, Wesley Davis, old Sturdivant and some of our other coloured families are as much a credit to your race as my Grandfather, Col. Fields; my father, Tom Fields and my Uncle, Grover Fields were to theirs. Rest assured yourself and hasten to assure your friends and neighbors that as long as the Fields blood beats in our veins we will devote ourselves to maintaining peace, comfort and propriety among those of you who have faithfully served us. To the others who have seen an opportunity in my father's death, my Mother's inexperience and my brothers' youth to make unfair gains for themselves, I have nothing but the toe of my boot but, for the faithful, hardworking Christian negro families, we have a home for as long as they live.

I could sense the proprietary nature of Dad's relationships with Matt and Charley Lee. How belittling, if not intimidating, these words must have felt to them. The deeply ingrained value system expressed in the letter had become old, tired, and even more wrong. Yet the letter indicated another dynamic of black/white relations. When I read this letter to a close black friend, she listened carefully and pointed out that racism in the South was very intimate and therefore, complex. She said that "there is a strain of decency here." A mutual dependence is apparent. "They 'have each other's backs.'" Dad acknowledges that while he is serving overseas, these men are invaluable. He exposes his vulnerability and asks for their help. Trust is understood and that trust is mutual. It has guaranteed them their right to be on the land. At twenty years of age, Dad is trying to be upright and moral, recognizing blacks as legitimate, but he is not giving up any power or agency to them.

❦

When my father's great-grandfather and his son, Harris Jesse, moved to the Delta in 1842, twenty-five years after Mississippi became a state, from Northampton County, North Carolina, he worked for a time as a day laborer and later as manager of the

Helena Plantation. Close by, the tiny settlement of McKinneyville would soon have a railroad. Early residents of the area received their mail by horseback every six weeks. Mr. McKinney built a boat landing on the Deer Creek so that goods could be delivered by paddleboat. It wasn't until 1884 that the railroad was built and not until 1913 that McKinneyville was incorporated and given the name Anguilla. My great-great-grandfather's frugal nature worked in his favor. Before too many years passed, he had enough money to buy a piece of land. The first registry of land indicates that in 1870, Jesse gave his son eighty acres.

Two slaves had relocated in the Delta with him. They and other local black folks became ready laborers. Jesse Rawles Fields had served as a slave patroller in North Carolina. An 1835 document describes his duties thus: To patrol his district every two weeks or so, to "arrest all runaways, suppress all thefts as they may have opportunity & power, also to take away all unlawful weapons, books and the like; and implicit a punishment of Fifteen stripes on all slaves they may find of their owners possessions without a proper permit or pass and a further punishment of twenty four stripes if they behave insolently." North Carolina slavery took place on large farms. It was reported to be far less brutal than in the Deep South, where there were more violent, mean-spirited overseers. In the Sharkey County, Mississippi, Courthouse, I found a musty leather volume titled *Marks and Brands*. Scanning it furtively to see if my family name appeared, I was relieved not to find it. Pages of names of slaves, their owners, and the physical markings that signified ownership turned my stomach. Most of those who were claimed as chattel bore branded insignia—numbers or initials—but some also had notches cut into their earlobes; for example, two 1914 entries read, "Right shoulder, right hip—brand" and "smooth crop in left ear and splits in right."

So the genesis of my family's pejorative view of African Americans went back to pre–Civil War days. Evidence of racism in succeeding generations became more subtle and underhanded. I learned by example from my grandmother and my father that blacks were inferior to whites. Though I shuddered when they expressed their prejudice overtly, I, like my kin, was negrophobic—stuck in a perpetual state of amnesia, fear, and secrecy. When I learned of the 1946 murders, however, I did not consider myself racist.

❧

My father had developed a heightened sense of responsibility the hard way. It was only eight years before he wrote his letter to Matt and Charley Lee, that his father, Thomas, died. On November 3, 1935, Mamaw had prepared a meal of fried oysters, shipped upriver from New Orleans. Afterwards they went to watch the boys play in a basketball game. Upon returning home, Thomas collapsed on the landing of the staircase at Greenfields and was rushed to Mercy Hospital in Vicksburg. There he was diagnosed with severe indigestion, and he was sent home. Mamaw made plans to put him on the train the following day at four in the afternoon heading for the Mayo Clinic, but he passed blood clots all night, suffered from unbearable pain, and in the wee hours of the morning succumbed to "coronary thrombosis." He left my grandmother with four children, 572 acres of the most fertile land in the world, a cotton gin, a property dispute with his family, and a vast hole in her heart. Her motto then, and always, was: Pick up and move on. She had had a premonition that her husband was going to die, and he, nineteen years older than she, had begun to prepare her. He taught her about farming, caring for an automobile, and managing finances.

Dad, the eldest, was thirteen when his father died. Uncle Tom, two years Dad's junior, reflected on this event in a journal his children asked him to write:

> I was standing in my bedroom window looking out at the hundreds of people in our front yard who had gathered for my father's funeral. I had just celebrated my eleventh birthday . . . and I was facing the first tragedy of my very young

life. With tears on my cheeks I said to God, "Why have you taken him away; the need for this man is great in this small community . . . you should have taken me!!" Immediately and for the first time in my life I heard the inner voice of the Holy Spirit say to me, "Do not cry, you will be with him again." Dad lay in his casket in our living room downstairs; the entire house was in a state of shock as friends from church and the community did what they could to comfort and give hope to all of us. We were a tight knit group in those depression days as we depended one on the other for survival. At the grave side an elderly black man came up to me and said, "What's we gonna do now, Mr. Tom?" I couldn't answer this elderly gentleman but suddenly I felt the weight of what he had asked regretting that at the time I was not yet a man. The family survived the next few years learning to accept the absence at the head of the table and adjusting to life as it came to us all.

After my grandfather was buried, Mamaw turned to my dad and said, "Jay, you are the head of this family now. I expect you to take your father's place." Just as he entered adolescence, he became scion of the family. But she'd had to stay on him, haranguing him to do tasks that she thought any thirteen-year-old could do. One day, he dropped a heavy wrought-iron bench that she asked him to move, and it broke into pieces. She never forgot that—his clumsiness, his lack of strength. Because this episode in Dad's life was one he repeated to me often, I knew it was a defining moment for him.

Before Dad's father died, he made Mamaw beneficiary of a forty-thousand-dollar life insurance policy, and he willed her the house and his half-interest in the gin. The land was left in an undivided estate. She went to Farmers and Merchants Bank in Vicksburg and cashed the insurance check. When her brother-in-law conspired to take over the gin, she took him to court. According to Mamaw, the judge was averse to ruling in favor of a woman, especially one with four young children, but when she opened her big black purse and poured the money out on the table, he changed his mind. That's the story Mamaw told me. Research suggests that there was an amicable swap. Mamaw traded Thomas's bank stock for Grover's interest in the gin.

᪥

While I tried to give myself some time to digest the uncovered story, I grew restless and distracted. It was more information than I could assimilate at one time. My mind continued to escape into the past. I reconstructed the early days of my parents' relationship. Before Dad's stint in the air force was terminated, he was sent to Boca Raton, Florida, to decompress. I found his discharge papers after he died and noted that he was diagnosed with "severe operational fatigue" and consequently was held at the base for eighteen days in October 1944. Doctors there tried to stimulate Dad to talk about his experiences in combat. He couldn't. Finally, they gave him sodium pentothal to open him up. It may have worked for a time, but it wasn't until the end of his life that he told me about this and about the horrors of war. He had watched many of his pilot friends' planes go down in enemy territory. Though he was stoic by nature, I doubt Dad could have shoved those memories down the well of permanent forgetfulness. When I asked my brother, Jay, about PTSD after World War II, he said, "Back then, it was take two aspirin, go home, sleep it off, you'll feel better in the morning—even though you were part of the machinery that killed twenty-three hundred people with bombs over a two-year period. That's okay, you'll be fine. You're a hero, you did the right thing."

Dad never mentioned the details I found on the back page of a yellowed resume. There he wrote of his military distinctions. "As pilot, aircraft commander, in the 12th and 15th Air Forces, he was awarded the Distinguished Flying Cross, the Air Medal with nine Oak Leaf Clusters and the Commanding General's Citation for Valor." Toward the end of his life when we sat on his back porch, as we often did, musing about the past, I asked him about the milestones of his journey. He didn't hesitate. "Graduation from flying school. Completion of combat missions and military service. It's been mostly downhill since then."

ॐ

Both my mother's parents and Mamaw had winter homes in Delray Beach, Florida, just a few miles from Boca Raton. My understanding is that Dad and Mom met in a tavern crowded with servicemen and young ingenues in the winter of 1945. In three months' time, they became engaged and were married in the enclosed garden of Mom's parents' winter house, standing on Tennessee soil shipped down for the occasion on June 13. It was a small wedding, with a few friends and family from both sides. The party was surrounded by pink-orange bougainvillea blossoms and avocado-laden trees. Mom was deeply in love with this handsome war hero, a pilot, decorated and esteemed among his peers for "excellent character."

Dad was Mom's ticket out of a grieving household. Her only brother had died in the air transport command while teaching new pilots how to "fly the hump" over the Himalayas and use oxygen. Joseph Henry Fleming III's plane crashed on the runway in Calcutta, full of soldiers hooking a ride home. There were too many men on board. The heavy plane lumbered down the runway, tried to lift off, got just so high, and then lost altitude and crashed. Everyone died. As soon as Mom's grandfather, John I. Cox, governor of Tennessee, heard this news, he called his lifelong friend, Secretary of State Cordell Hull, and asked him to get the details. Uncle Joe's body was not recovered but a burial took place in Calcutta. Then my grandparents had his gravesite moved to Hawaii where a casket filled with sand was interred.

For Dad, the death of Mom's brother held mystery and fed his fascination with the Indian Raj and the caste system, which was akin to the feudal state that existed in Mississippi when he was a boy, and even in 1945. While playing hide-and-seek when he was eleven, my father discovered a twelve-volume set of the complete works of Kipling, bound in red Moroccan leather, beneath his parents' bed. Long before his birthday that year, Dad surreptitiously read the entire set. He wrote, years later, "I think if I could have chosen a second life for myself, it would have been as a young subaltern reporting to a British regiment a la John Masters in *Bugles and a Tiger.*" Henceforth, when Dad, Tom, Bill, and Sis engaged in baseball games with hand-wound string balls and homemade bats, when they placed pennies on the railroad tracks across Highway 61 from Mamaw's house, and when they dug trenches and hid in them, his siblings called him "Lord Beaverbrook."

⚶

Jay phoned me at home. "Molly, I'm still intrigued and need some answers."

"Me, too."

"There might not be anything more to this than Dad acting in self-defense. But I can't stop thinking about the man who was shot. Somehow, I would like to make it up to his family."

I hadn't considered that angle. "Well, it happened a long time ago. It's probably too late, but I do wonder if he left behind a wife and children."

"I bet Mamaw paid for this in more ways than one."

"I just don't want to let the story grow cold again, not without knowing the truth. As soon as I can, I'm going to Mississippi."

"I'll go with you," Jay said. And I was glad for that.

CHAPTER FOUR

My Mother's Version

April 2006

While I prepared to make my first return visit to Mississippi since my grandmother died in 1984, my focus shifted once again to the past. I became engrossed in reconstructing my parents' early married years in Mississippi. After the war, Dad returned to the Delta to step into his father's farming boots. But he was not cut out to be a farmer. Dad was a thinker who delighted in language and ideas. He balked at the family business, borrowed money from Mamaw and the bank and bought the *Deer Creek Pilot,* a weekly newspaper serving three counties. His first issue was dated May 3, 1946, seven months before the incident. The office was located in Rolling Fork, a slightly larger town than Anguilla, only five miles away from the plantation. As publisher, editor, advertising manager, pressman, printer, linotype machine operator, reporter, and janitor, he was engaged and happy with his work. He thrived on opportunities to track down stories and hobnob with reporters and editors at other regional papers. He wrote about hot topics like the weak governor of Mississippi, cultural concerns, farming, and problems related to prohibition of alcohol.

Mamaw's house was set back from the highway and surrounded by hundreds of flat acres of cotton plants. Identical white clapboard houses—one on each side of the "big" house—sat closer to the road. My parents moved into one; the manager of the cotton gin leased the other. While Dad was off newspapering, Mom tried to settle herself in this foreign soil. The little town of Anguilla had a population of around eight hundred, 75 percent of whom were black. The main area of commerce was composed of a bank, two stores, the Prestiani Barber Shop, an elementary school, an icehouse, the post office, and the train depot. The town had little to offer a young woman of twenty-two who had lived for a time in New York City.

Mom didn't start off on the right foot with my grandmother. The enmity that grew between them was a mystery to me for most of my life, though I could understand how Mom might have chafed at Mamaw's domination and her strict adherence to the protocol of plantation life.

Long after Mamaw died, Mom and I were chatting about the past. The corners of her mouth lifted, her eyes twinkled and she looked down—just like a child who had successfully pilfered a cookie behind her mother's back. The following story emerged:

Soon after Mom and Dad married in Delray Beach, Florida, May 1945, they drove away from the Sunbelt, from the lovely winter home of Mom's parents and from all that was familiar to Mom, to Mississippi. Under a relentless Delta summer sun, Mom set about the task of making a home for herself and the man she was still madly in love with while my grandmother went to work planning a bridge party, which would be the scene of Mom's "coming out" in lower Delta society.

The gathering of plantation owners' wives and daughters was set to take place at the home of Mrs. Carpenter. There would have been a lavish buffet set out on the dining room table with linens, polished silverware, china plates and serving dishes, crystal goblets, candelabra with dangling prisms, and a massive bouquet of fresh cut flowers from the ladies' gardens. Mamaw would have dressed in her finest, perhaps a navy blue belted dress with matching jacket, shoes, and purse—all of which she would have purchased on a semiannual trip to Memphis or New Orleans. She would have worn her diamond broach on the outside (not pinned to her bra), pearls, and white kid gloves. This was, after all, the first marriage in her brood—something to celebrate. After dressing herself, she would have fussed over Sis and then the two of them would have driven south on Highway 61 to Rolling Fork, arriving early so as to assist the hostess. After the black kitchen help made finger sandwiches of cucumber slices and cream cheese, dropped snipped dill onto the surface of a chilled potato soup, and sliced fresh fruit—strawberries, watermelon, black-berries—Mamaw might have helped arrange the table, carefully placing freshly polished silver bowls and platters on the cutwork tablecloth laundered by the help.

My mother was not unschooled in social graces. She was descended from three state governors: Alexander Spottswood, governor of Virginia for the Crown in 1710, John Isaac Cox, governor of Tennessee in 1905, and Gabriel Moore, fifth governor of Alabama, 1829. I have Gabriel's photograph, which was tucked inside a small box with Mom's mother's written note, dated 1954: "This portrait is painted on ivory and was given to me by my mother who had kept it for me. I want Betsy Fields to have it and in turn Miss Mollie Fields." Pride was plentiful on Mom's side of the family.

Her parents, Mary and Joe Fleming, were among the privileged in their town of Bristol, Tennessee. They wore their financial and social entitlements with confidence and graciousness. Mom and her brother, Joe, before his death in World War II, were accustomed to formal social events, were well-mannered and courteous. When Mom recounted her bridge party story, it didn't take me long to figure out the faux pas that created a rift between her and Mamaw.

ჿჄჿ

"I was at home that Saturday, just piddling around, when the phone rang around noon. The voice on the other end, an older lady's voice, asked me what I was doing. Instantly, I remembered that there was a party for me that day."

"Mom . . . what did you do?"

"Well, I jumped in the shower, washed my hair and shoved in some bobby pins. I threw on my dress and drove to Rolling

Fork. When I got there, my hair was still wet." But getting dressed in those days was a complicated thing. Mom would have had to shimmy into a girdle and pull on a pair of silk hose. That would have upped her body temperature on a simmering day. She had perspiration guards, folded and stitched muslin patches that were cut to fit in the crease of the armpit, thus protecting the dress layer from sweaty skin. Her dress, one from her trousseau, would have been purchased by Mam (her mother) at some boutique on Worth Avenue in Palm Beach and may have needed a bit of pressing, but there was no time to take it to the big house so that Jo could iron out the creases. If she'd taken the time to brush on a layer of fingernail polish, that would have further postponed her arrival. No doubt her hostesses delayed lunch and made small talk—never alluding to the fact that the honoree was not there.

"You just forgot? About the party?"

That same sneaky grin came back. "I just completely forgot."

I can only imagine the deep embarrassment my grandmother would have felt when Mom didn't arrive on time. That she came with wet hair still pinned up would have distressed her to no end. Mom's little omission was a slap in the face that would smart for the rest of Mamaw's life. It is probable, maybe even likely, that Mom wanted to impress upon her new mother-in-law the fact that social events in that godforsaken place couldn't hold a candle to those she had experienced in her childhood home.

Try as she could to dampen my fervent love for Mamaw, Mom was never successful. My grandmother's overt, physical, and unconditional expressions of love fell like manna on the heart of a little girl who could not see the flaws in that loving presence. Mamaw was perfect, and because of my unflagging love, I was not able to see her degrading treatment of her servants as a sign of racism.

⚭

While I was charting my trip to the Delta, it dawned on me that maybe Sis was right. Maybe I needed to call Mom before I left, to see what she might add. I was reluctant to phone her because we had been at a benign impasse for several months. I had failed to anticipate how my move to Asheville was going to upset my mother's plans for us. And I didn't feel comfortable phoning her about an incident loaded with painful memories. But after thinking about it, my curiosity overcame circumspection, and I called her in Cookeville, Tennessee, where she lived three blocks from my sister. I felt tense and wary. She was normally curt and guarded with me in the best of times. My vulnerability pushed me into a supplicant position—never a good idea with Mom, but after a few minutes of small talk, she was willing to open up about it.

"Molly, I felt like it was just something you kids didn't need to know about. But now that you do, I can tell you the *real* story. You see, Jay was born in October and the thing happened soon after that. Bill went to the train station to pick up Sis when she arrived home from college. A black man flirted with her and that didn't sit well with your uncle. Later that night, Bill, Tom, and your father went to the saloon to straighten things out. They'd been drinking." I thought of Emmett Till who was murdered for alleged flirtation with a white woman in 1955.

She told me that she was at home nursing Jay, when the sheriff came to the door with Dad. It was a terrifying moment when he told her what Dad had done. "The way I heard it, a black man tried to get the gun away from your dad." She finished her story by saying, "I never told this to anybody."

"Mom, this must have been so scary for you."

She didn't respond but went on. "I thought I was in love with your father at the time. It was the hardest thing I have ever had to do in my life—call my parents and tell them that their new son-in-law was in jail for manslaughter. They didn't understand. Your dad was only in jail for a night or two. He should have been put in prison."

Though her last statement stunned me with its harsh implications, maybe Mom was right.

"But why did Dad have a gun?"

Again, she avoided my question and said, "The whole time we were in Mississippi, I was scared to death. I felt like a misfit down there. It was like living in a foreign country. Things happened I just couldn't believe. Oh, my lord, no wonder I've had ulcers and depression all my life. My stomach is hurting right now." Her voice became harder than usual, so I felt she must be angry at me for broaching the subject. I, too, felt a sinking feeling in my gut. This story about Dad was not going to be as easy to put to bed as I had thought.

Before she got off the line, Mom told me that Hodding Carter and his wife, Betty, drove down from Greenville to Anguilla to visit her and interview her about the shooting right after it happened. I wondered if Mom had any idea of Carter's battle for equality between the races in the Delta. She knew he was owner and editor of the Greenville *Delta Democrat Times*, but I doubt she was aware of his determination to bring about change to the caste-based system that was being defended so vigorously by wealthy farmers like my dad's family, or that Carter won a Pulitzer Prize for his crusade. I checked my history books to see exactly how progressive he was. What I found was that Carter's work began more than ten years before the boycott of buses in Montgomery, Alabama, before Martin Luther King, Jr., spoke with a new voice that called for reason, dignity, and sanity.

Mom stayed in her marriage to Dad for thirty years, divorcing him in 1975. After that, she rankled at the mention of any of my father's family members, bitter that they had not remained loyal to her. She expected them to correspond with her and to care about her life. Though fairly newly divorced, even I knew that family relations didn't work that way. In a voice thick with sarcasm, she suggested that I call Sis. I recognized this as an attempt to cut the phone call short.

"I did. Sis said that Mamaw was entertaining some folks from Kentucky."

"She was. It was the Thomases. Beck only knew them because Mother and Daddy introduced them at my wedding. They were old, old family friends. And they left Anguilla the minute they got word of what your father had done. I almost died of embarrassment. I need a glass of wine. I'll talk to you later."

I looked at my watch. Sure enough . . . it was five o'clock. Cocktail hour. If I'd waited any longer, I probably would have heard a much more elaborate and nuanced, yet less trustworthy tale.

Mom told me that she would have left Dad when he was charged, but the only exit route was to take her small child to her parents' home. Mam and Joe were still grieving the death of their son, Joe, and my grandfather was recovering from a serious heart attack as well. Going home was not an option for Mom.

I made note of what she said. Already I had three different versions of what happened that December night, Tommy's, Sis's, and Mom's. Clearly, no one telling of the story would be completely true. Any retelling of what happened in the past would contain ambiguities. It was time for me to start searching for answers outside the family. I decided to check for newspaper accounts. It was doubtful that Dad had covered his own story in the *Deer Creek Pilot*, and later I discovered that he had not. The code of silence was fully in place. I decided to contact the *Delta Democrat Times*. There were no issues that old in the archives at the paper. I was sent to Greenville's Percy Library and then to a researcher.

I contacted the Rolling Fork police department where Sheriff Crawford worked in 1946. Shyly, I asked the operator for records of the shooting. She gave me the number for city hall in Anguilla. Again, I was deflected, this time to the Sharkey County clerk's office. "Too long ago," I kept hearing. "Try the circuit clerk's office."

"We do have some very old record books but they are not computerized. I'm sorry, but you will have to go through them by hand." When the clerk said this, it landed in my stomach like a stone. Out of the recesses of my mind came a feeling that I had known for a long time, that one day I would be making a trip to Mississippi to look for clues to something. I just didn't quite know what.

Finally, the researcher called me back. "I have a feeling this needle is in a very big haystack. I did notice on the World War II enlistment forms your dad stated his occupation was motion picture film actor/director/writer. Was he in Hollywood at some point? Just curious."

Oh, here we go . . . typical Dad . . . always up to high jinks. I thought back to my high school days when he took delight in embarrassing me in front of my friends. Often he answered the phone, "Ah so! Chang's Chinese Laundry." My friends either hung up on him or heard the humor in his voice and played along.

Meanwhile, it was becoming clear to me that this secret had subverted any semblance of normalcy in my family. At fifty-seven, despite the best efforts of numerous therapists, I had only just begun to piece together my childhood—to get a bead on the nature of our family's dysfunction, to cast my parents in permanent human roles. I had given up on figuring out the enigma that was my father, and I had etched what I thought was a detailed picture of my parents, their problems and their personalities. Now, suddenly, everything had to be reexamined. I felt ambiguity and ambivalence. And anger—anger at Dad for causing me to reopen old family wounds. More questions surfaced. What really happened and who was guilty of what? What made him angry or fearful enough to take another man's life? How did my grandmother handle all of this?

Then, somehow, in the middle of this huge thing, a new insight came to me. This story, however strange, could be very valuable. I started to feel lighter. I started to feel free. Just maybe, what I had felt growing up, in the tense and confusing ether of our home, was not there because of my failing, my shame. Maybe it had nothing to do with me.

On Saturday night, April 22, the phone rang. It was my researcher in Greenville. "I found the newspaper accounts—right when the library was closing. It looks like your daddy was charged with man-slaughter. He was released on five housand dollars bond. There was a grand jury hearing February of '47, but I haven't found anything on that yet. Anyway, this happened in December of '46 and there were two men shot, not one. The bylines seem to be aimed at keeping this quiet and out of the racial arena. I'll send these to you."

Wed., Dec. 18, 1946 *Delta Democrat Times*.
Headline: Anguilla Tragedy Not Racial Clash. Subhead:
Clean-Up was Editor's Aim.

ROLLING FORK—Sheriff C. D. Crawford of Sharkey county said today that manslaughter charges had been preferred against H. J. Fields, 24-year old Air Forces veteran and editor of the *Deer Creek Pilot*, in connection with the slaying of two Negroes at Anguilla, five miles from here, last Thursday night. The Negroes were David Jones and Simon Toombs, both of Anguilla.

Sheriff Crawford said that "it is my understanding that Mr. Fields and his two brothers were attempting to influence several white operators of beer and dance joints for Negroes to close their establishments." He also said that he did not believe that Mr. Fields had intended to accost anyone except the white operators. Earlier this month a petition for the closing of establishments had been circulated by Anguilla citizens without success.

Released Under Bond

Mr. Fields, who lives in Anguilla, but who publishes in Rolling Fork the weekly newspaper, which he purchased after being discharged from the Air Forces, declined to make any statement. He was released under $5,000 bond last Friday to await action of the grand jury in February.

No action was taken against Mr. Fields' brothers, Tom and Billy, also veterans. Tom Fields was wounded during the affray.

Sheriff's Statement

Sheriff Crawford's statement follows:

"On last Thursday evening, rather early in the night, I was called to Anguilla, a town in Sharkey county by Town Marshall O. O. Wanker to investigate trouble that had occurred there.

"When I reached there I found that David Jones and Simon Toombs, Negroes, had been killed by Mr. H. J. Fields, of Anguilla, in a shooting affray, during an altercation and struggle with the Negroes that took place on the main street of town.

"Both Negroes were shot once each, as their bodies showed, in the front. I then arrested Mr. Fields and brought him to Rolling Fork. The following day, a charge of manslaughter was made against Mr. Fields, and being a bailable case, bond in the amount of $5,000 was fixed and Mr. Fields was released.

No Racial Issues

"It is my understanding that they were attempting to influence several white operators of beer and dance joints for Negroes to close their establishments. There was no evidence that Mr. Fields had been drinking or that he had intended to accost anyone but the white operators.

"None of the participants were attached to the sheriff's office nor was there any evidence that racial issues were involved."

A double murder! Oh, God, no! It was bad enough that one human life ended that night. But two? I had to fight with myself to keep from transforming Dad's image from that of a citizen on a do-good mission to that of a vigilante in a white robe, head covered, preparing to burn crosses or lynch an innocent black man. How could this possibly be! I stood frozen, mouth agape, eyes wide open. I had hoped that it was, truly, a case of self-defense, that Tommy's details about the stolen car were accurate. But how could it be that two men were dead? The questions piled up. I was too far away from the scene to get the answers. I would have to go to Mississippi.

CHAPTER FIVE

The New Mississippi

May 18, 2006

It was a beautiful spring in Asheville in May, two months after Uncle Tom died, as I prepared to go to Mississippi and find out the real story of the shoot-out. When I moved here in 2001, I bought a new arts and crafts–style bungalow that fit with the art deco architecture of the city. It was situated on a hillside facing south toward mountains. From the front porch rockers I could sit and stare into forested slopes. Often Jay came over for dinner, and we sat outside way past dusk until we were starving for real food, not just pistachios, crackers, and cheese. We talked about Dad mostly, but Jay was still focusing on the aftereffects the murder had on the dead men's families. I was caught up in the details of the scene, fascinated and repulsed at the same time. It would be many months before a truer version would take shape in my mind. But I was driven to dig. The story had a hold on my imagination. I could envision Dad, Tom, and Bill sitting in Mamaw's living room, the three of them dressed for dinner wearing sport coats and dress shirts but no ties. Dad would likely have been smoking a pipe and knocking back a cocktail, telling what happened in the war. Tom might have been relating the experience of sitting in the bubble under the plane, his finger on the trigger of a machine gun when the Japs appeared out of nowhere. But Bill's concerns would have leaned towards farming, the weather, the price of cotton, the emboldened black servicemen who he thought were spending too much time in the tavern in town drinking themselves senseless. It was clear that military training had the potential to reduce if not extinguish a man's ability to care about human life outside of his own beloved. Add that perspective to a southern white farmer's views on race and that's when real trouble could set in.

While I tucked my clothes and personal articles into a duffle, new fears began to make themselves known in my body. My throat tightened as the thoughts came—*what if I stir up something buried in the dust, something that could inflame new racial tensions? What if I discover other family secrets while I am there? Will this quicksand swallow me whole? Might I find out that I am not the person I've thought myself to be?*

Remembering the idyllic hours I spent in Mississippi each summer for years helped to settle me. Mamaw drove the many miles to Tennessee to get Jay and me. We spent two wonderful weeks at her house being kids, playing in the giant magnolia tree, catching frogs on the front stoop at night, secreting ourselves in what seemed like a giant plantation house as our father and his siblings had done. In my travels as an adult to Europe, India, Mexico, even this broad country we call home, I have never experienced any place capable of evoking the sensual delight of a waning summer day in the Mississippi Delta.

๑อ๑

Jay and I were to leave Asheville after Sunday church and drive part of the way. But the trip started with an hour delay, not unusual for Jay, who hasn't been on time a day in his life. He hadn't packed. His clothes were still in the dryer. "Would you fold them for me?" He wanted me to see the new walking trail he carved through the woods beside his house. He wanted me to give ample attention to Miles (as in Davis), his cat. And he needed time to get his gear in order while we listened to a new jazz CD. This delay took me back to the many Sunday mornings when Mom, Dad, Laura, and I waited in the car for Jay to come out of the house so we could get on our way to church. It never failed. He emerged wearing only his trousers and carrying shirt, jacket, tie, shoes, and socks in his hands—hair still wet from the shower. Then Laura and I had to squiggle around in the back seat to allow him space to finish dressing. On this day, forty some years later, I made a decision that I would not let a backwash of frustration spoil this trip. It was an adventure, and I wanted to keep it that way. With heedless abandon, I was launching on a journey that promised to be bigger than anything I had yet experienced, and I hadn't a clue about the consequences or the deep inner work that was soon to be required of me.

Our first destination was Greenville, Mississippi. I wanted to see the newspaper article from the *Delta Democrat Times* and look for other clues. After we skirted Memphis, Highway 61 unsnaked itself into long, flat miles through millions of rows of fresh yellow-green cotton plants, corn, and soybeans emerging from their spring planting. The sky held up an occasional stratus cloud against a cobalt background. In atypical seventy-degree weather, it was a pleasant drive, and we marveled at the levees that rose beside the Mississippi River. Gaudy casinos became more frequent along the way. The occasional crop duster took off from a dirt and gravel airstrip and buzz-bombed a chemical potion onto the farms below. When we arrived in Greenville, it was as if we were wading into the great swamp of deep southern culture tainted by the blight of urban decay.

Jay and I talked out various scenarios of what happened those many years ago. We had three versions of the story now plus a newspaper account. We talked about our children; both of us divorced, both with two grown daughters at differing stages in their development as young women. We talked about good movies we'd seen and books we'd read. I was happy to have some time with Jay. He was comfortable and easy. But in the course of driving eight hundred miles, I realized that he had framed a story with a larger scope—one that he could live with, one that he did not expect to have overturned. Even though Jay was open to discovery, he wasn't expecting any sort of definitive answer to surface. One of his more recent girlfriends told me, "Jay is steeped in his own sort of mythos." I was not ready for a definitive answer to sum up Dad's culpability either, but I needed for there to be something in his actions that shed light on my relationship with him. I had hope that we would come to know the truth. I thought I was keeping an open mind.

❦

Several roads led into downtown Greenville. Somehow, I chose the less scenic one that took us by hamburger row, dumpy tire stores, and a used car lot. We emerged into what had been a historic, central business district with old southern architecture alongside 1960s-era brick government buildings. We drove to the levee on the west side of town where two or three brightly lit casinos pressed up against the bank of the river. Fifty years ago, casinos near city centers would have been unthinkable. We found a Fairfield Inn and registered.

The receptionist at the hotel suggested that Doe's Eat Place was our best bet for dinner. Around 6:00 p.m., we started walking from the library to Nelson Street. I was aware of the steady, standoffish gazes of the residents in the neighborhood we passed through. Two black men sat on a bench near the front door of Doe's, eyeing us as we approached. I felt my body tense as we drew near. Maybe coming here wasn't such a good idea. When we entered the kitchen door and met Doe's wife, a pleasant white woman with a colorful apron around her rotund body, she asked, "Y'all didn't walk here, did ya?" Not happy with my answer she said, "You're not from around here, where are you stayin'? Cause I'm gonna drive you to your hotel after supper. It's not safe to walk around here."

Doe started his family restaurant in 1941, when he turned his father's grocery into a kitchen and started frying up crawfish and steaks the size of Texas. It is on the main street of the black neighborhood. He opened a juke joint in the front of the store, blacks only, and the whites arrived at the back door by carriage and had their own private restaurant. The dining room where we were seated looked as it must have for the past sixty years. Jay and I ordered beer and looked around at the plastic tablecloths, posters of B. B. King, photos of cotton fields in bloom, and framed articles from *Life* magazine and the *Arkansas Times*.

"I've been here before," Jay said in a reminiscent sort of way.

"Really, when?"

"Back when Dad and I came down to go dove hunting with Uncle Bill and Uncle Tom."

"I remember seeing photos of that trip in Dad's apartment."

"Yeah, it was great. The tamales are what they're famous for."

Ironically, we were sitting in the back room, behind what was once a juke jive operated by "Big Doe" in the 1940s. He had gone into bootlegging to help recover financially after the flood of 1927.

I wondered what was keeping this shack-like building from collapsing after so many years, but in a few minutes, southern "juice" began to seep into my skin. Two men sat talking at a table in the corner. Everyone who came in was white. They eyed us and then smiled. It felt like yesterday when I last walked into my grandmother's kitchen and asked Aunt Mat for a glass of milk.

On the way back to the hotel, Doe's wife talked about the tragedy of her hometown. She gave us a "white" perspective on the state of this historic Mississippi city. "We are hopin' that Greenville is gonna come back. We're 75 percent black now, and everybody with school-aged kids spends their last dime sending them to private school. The casinos have ruined our life here. We have gangs and street violence and drugs. Eighty percent of the money that goes into those casinos is government money—social security checks and welfare. I know some fine, upstandin' people who have had to move far away from here because of gamblin' addiction." She shook her head.

Maybe the spoils of fighting a war against racism in the Deep South had created a power shift so that now whites carried fear in their hearts. This thought made me more uncomfortable than I already was.

The next morning I got up early enough to take a walk along the levee. As I crested the hill, I could see Jay jogging in the distance. He was fifty-nine and a good athlete. "Molly, it's possible to stay as fit as an eighteen-year-old when you're way past fifty," he'd told me many times. I knew that he maintained his regimen because of polycystic kidney disease and because of his desire to keep his weight under control. I had struggled with weight problems off and on, myself, just as our father and grandmother had. Twenty-five years of practicing and teaching yoga had kept my body supple, strong, and healthy. But I had never been happy with my body image. Jay interrupted my musings, and we stood, staring at the beauty of the Mississippi River, cypress groves standing in deep water with bulky root systems, stretched-out fields, the warmth of the sun, and the anticipation of getting down to Anguilla gave me a sense of mission and purpose. Though I felt I knew this part of the country by heart, somehow it seemed as if the heart had gone out of it.

After breakfast, Jay and I took the advice of several people and stopped by McCormick Book Inn on our way out of town. Hugh McCormick greeted us warmly and led us through stacks of local and regional history books, southern novels and biographies. He further elaborated on the state of affairs in Mississippi.

"The infrastructure decline in the Delta has made these south Delta counties the poorest in the poorest state in the nation. The best and brightest can't stay here now."

I had the feeling Hugh already knew about us before we got there but he asked anyway, "Where are you from? What brings you to the Delta?"

Jay deferred to me and I recounted the story about our dad, wincing and noting that it felt more uncomfortable to tell a stranger than to tell someone who had known my family in the past.

The phone rang and I heard Hugh say, "You better come on over here."

Then he continued to walk us through his extensive inventory. I was captivated by the unique atmosphere and rich patina of an older bookstore. I'd visited numerous independents in the '90s before I opened shop in my hometown. This was the epitome of what I'd envisioned for Book Ends. Sadly, it didn't have the staying power to survive hard economic times, and, after five years, I closed the doors.

Hugh wore khakis with a white button-down shirt and suspenders; he had graying hair and intense eyes. He became more and more animated and excited about his titles as he spoke. I picked up a copy of *The Most Southern Place on Earth* and he said, "That is probably one of the most important books we have that tells about how things got to be the way they are. That, and *Lanterns on the Levee* by William A. Percy."

Within two or three minutes his impish middle-aged wife, Mary Dayle, bounced in the door, grinning wide. She pulled on a deep southern drawl and smothered us in "y'all" and "Lord a mercy."

We talked briefly about the changes in Greenville. As she spoke, Mary Dayle's speech was accentuated with lavish gestures. She was one of the most animated people I had ever talked with. "There are shootings every weekend in the streets and somebody burned a house down last month and there's drug dealings and . . . We all shop at the same stores no matter what our backgrounds, education, or income. We all go to the same doctors, and we use the same services and we travel the same streets. We don't have segregated neighborhoods like they do in big cities so we're not insulated from one another. We're in each other's faces all the time and so we are aware of each other, and we are forced to get along so it seems like there's a lot of friction, but I don't think it is any more friction than in an extended family. It's just that they can't get away from me and I can't get away from them . . . with a capital "T" whether they are the rednecks or the hostile blacks or the Mexicans that don't speak English."

I thought, these people are still wading through the backwash of years of racial discrimination that began before my family even settled in Mississippi.

She turned, dialed the phone, and spoke to her mother, once a resident of Rolling Fork. She listened and then replied, "Mama says, 'Oh, for the Lord's sake. Those Fields boys raised some hell but it was good for 'em.'"

Whoa, she knew Mom and Dad.

Then Mary Dayle handed the phone to me.

Her mother, Trudy, said, "You were a baby and when oh, less see that was—oh lord, that was in '48 or '49. And oh you were a sweet thing. Oh, I'd give anything to see y'all. Is your mama still livin'?"

"Yes ma'am, she's in Cookeville where my sister lives."

"Uh-hunh. Is she still wearin' high heels and smokin' cigarettes?"

We both laughed and I said, "Oh, of course." But that wasn't the truth. Later, I thought about my response and wondered why I felt a need to laugh and answer with a lie. Clearly, I was anxious and tense about what lay ahead of me.

"What was your husband's name?" I asked her.

"Jack Schultz. Jack did a lot of photography and all back then. Just the other day someone came lookin' for some of his pictures. Well, the film was horrible then, and we had it in our grain elevator which didn't help. The pictures are all gone."

We had chitchatted long enough. I mustered the courage to ask her about the shooting in Anguilla.

"I remember the Fields boys closing up a honky-tonk. Tom was hotheaded. Bill just kind of went along. And your daddy was gonna try to argue his way. He was the one hell-bent for leather on things like that. I don't recall them killin' anybody. They might have shot 'em or whatever but I do remember the incident, and I wouldn't want to be quoted on it because I lived in Rolling Fork and I just heard about it. Whatever it was, it was shut up. That's the way things were done then."

The conversation ebbed and we hung up. Jay and I spent $184 between us on books we thought might give us more context and history. We said good-bye to the McCormicks and headed south on Highway 61. Before we left, Hugh suggested we go first to the office of the *Deer Creek Pilot* in Rolling Fork.

Around 11:00, we pulled into Rolling Fork. Only slightly larger than Anguilla, its population was about fifteen hundred. A handful of streets had retained a smattering of large, well-maintained homes and yards. On the extreme ends of the streets, ten to twelve blocks out from city center, were shacks. These rusty tin-roofed houses, some with precious little paint, porches made of scrap lumber, windows and doors hanging on their hinges, old barrels and odd containers scattered in the front yards, were still occupied. The residents couldn't make much more than a hand-to-mouth living.

Jay and I looked for the homes of families we knew growing up. I spotted Mimi Courtright's house. She was Mamaw's bosom (and buxom) buddy. Together they chaperoned a group of five high school graduates to Europe for five weeks. I was one of them. Seeing the row of houses facing a dried-up section of Deer Creek, we recalled hot afternoons walking from town under the tall oak trees and swaying willows, crossing over the bridges, and cooling off in the all-white swimming pool with its algaed water.

Next, we stopped at a cemetery to look for names on tomb-stones, and we photographed a hand-sized, pearly white magnolia blossom. Maybe we were procrastinating about going to the next destination. Maybe we were ruminating about a distant past, one we knew less about than we ever thought. But as I stood there, looking out beyond headstones into the rows of cotton plants, the smell of loamy soil gave me a sense of home, slowed me down, reminded me of a much simpler, gentrified life—simpler, anyway, for white people like me. Jay, in his slow ways, ambled around the grounds, taking into his senses the feel of being there. I admired the way he stayed quietly in the moment, absorbing all it had to offer him.

ॐ

Slight and wiry and outspoken like many newspaper editors, Ray Mosby welcomed us into the small white house where he worked with two assistants. He made space for us at a conference table in what used to be a dining room so that we could leaf through two years of musty bound issues that were printed in Dad's four-year tenure as owner of the *Deer Creek Pilot*. Jay and I didn't explain why we were there. But over the next two hours we pored, knowing there would be nothing written about the dead men or Dad's involvement.

Jay leafed through the yellowed and brittle pages too fast for me. "Slow down. I don't want to miss anything." He was probably impatient with me, too, for tarrying in the society pages. I saw the names of Mr. and Mrs. Jack Schultz and thought about the conversation I had with Trudy just that morning in Greenville. There were family names as well. I saw an announcement that Aunt Sis was home from Stephens College for Thanksgiving, and that so-and-so had driven to Vicksburg for the day. Reading the papers gave me a sense of the tight community of white farmers and businessmen that lived in the three counties covered by the paper. Jack Dayle Shultz's photographs were peppered through the pages.

While we read, Ray rattled on about the area. "I have a theory—when I was a kid, when you went to the big city, if you lived in the north Delta, you went to Memphis. If you lived in the south Delta, you went to Jackson, and Memphis is infinitely more culturally sophisticated than is Jackson, and I think when Tommy and Susie go to college, in the north, they go to Ole Miss and in the south they go to State, and Ole Miss is simply way more sophisticated because of Oxford. I'm not saying it's better but it's different. It's more culturally inclined."

During those hours of turning pages, we ran across three editorials on alcoholism that Dad wrote. One was a response to a call by the Mississippi Baptist Convention president to elect prohibitionists in the fall of that year. On November 22, just a few weeks before the shoot-out, Dad wrote:

> I have no fear of the effects of alcohol IF all alcohol is brought out of its cloistered element and placed in the clear cold light of sound reasoning. For too long the American public has placed the traffic in alcohol in a closet like a family half-wit who must be kept from close scrutiny. Like

toadstools, mold and scum the improper handling of this commodity has grown to such proportions that the bad effects have been overshadowed by the filth and corruptness with which it is handled. The filthy juke joint, the brothel, the gambling den, the pimp, the whore, the bootlegger, the corrupt politician, the phony cures for alcoholics, the petty racketeers grew from efforts to abolish the sale of alcohol and from no other reason. There is only one way to fight the bootlegger and that is to make legal the traffic in the article with which he deals and use the profit which he is getting now to combat the effects of his product.

These words and others on issues of community concern helped me to visualize my father at work, writing passionately about the issues he saw as important. Also, I began to see how angry Dad was that the juke joints in and around Anguilla were interfering with farm work. In the weeks prior to the shoot-out, a band of citizens had circulated a petition to close establishments where alcohol was sold illegally. Nothing had come of those efforts.

ᘒ

Around 3:00 in the afternoon, Jay and I drove to the Rolling Fork square where the yellow brick Sharkey County Circuit Court-house stood like an isle in a bay. Pat Thrasher, deputy clerk, showed us to the docket room. She directed us to the shelves of thick, red leather volumes of court recordings. While she looked for 1946 and '47, Jay drifted over to a seven-foot-tall framed map dating back to 1905. There he located plots of land with the name "H. J. Fields" inscribed on them. He asked me to take his picture, pointing at the areas with his pen.

Through later research I found out that in 1861, my great-grandfather, Harris, whose father, Jesse Rawles, first settled in the Delta, enlisted as a private in Company L of the Mississippi cavalry under the command of General Wirt Adams. The first combat that he participated in was at Bowling Green, Kentucky, but they retreated from there to Nashville and fought in the bloody Battle of Shiloh. He stayed with his regiment through several engagements but ended up in Alabama when the final surrender of the South occurred. Paroled in May 1865, he traveled to New Orleans, signed on with a keelboat and poled up the Sunflower River toward home. His willing participation in one of the bloodiest wars in history had to have affected my father, and inspired his courage when he shipped out to Africa to fly planes for the Allied forces in World War II. It is ironic that while my great-great-grandfather fought for the right to continue to enslave his black workers, my father fought to set free the oppressed people in Europe.

Sometime later, I found Harris Jesse's obituary in my father's baby book. It read, "By energy, thrift and far-sightedness he amassed a fortune." First he had to deforest the land and sell the wood before he could start to put together a significant holding, a place where his family and his black workers could settle and prosper.

I watched as Pat Thrasher leafed through the yellowed docket books with beautiful handwritten accounts of misdeeds and serious offenses, like stealing another man's mule. When we looked through the grand jury cases for 1947, there was nothing to be found on the Fields versus Anguilla saloon case.

"Please, is there any other documentation that we might find here?"

Pat looked at me with kindness and remained silent while she searched her mind. This middle-aged, white clerk, who had snapshots of grandchildren around her desk, knew the legal terrain. First, she went to her phone and called the sheriff's department. Then she phoned the district attorney's office in Vicksburg. There were no records on file that dated back that far. We would have to content ourselves with a slew of secondhand, word-of-mouth accounts. I thanked her and we left the courthouse.

Dejected, I was beginning to wonder whether our search was getting us anywhere or whether the trip down was even worth it. Maybe I should just accept the composite story at face value and recognize that what happened was just "the way it was back then." But I really couldn't let it go at that. So, though it was late in the afternoon, Jay and I drove the five miles to Anguilla. The town was a mere cluster of buildings, some empty. As we eased down the main street past the bank, city hall, and post office, the straight road made a sharp turn to the left and almost immediately straightened out again. I had a cinematic experience when my body shifted with the curve. "This is the way to Mamaw's house," and I breathed in a sigh that took me all the way back, some fifty years, into the mind and memory of a little, dark-haired girl who adored her grandmother. I remembered the smell of Elizabeth Arden, the confident voice of a teacher of "expression," the swish of a fan against the noon heat, the bead of rosy color that came to her lips when she pursed them together applying her lipstick, the sight of her generous backside as she clipped enough red, yellow, and orange zinnias from her garden to warm the dinner table. Though dead for twenty-one years, she was as alive in my mind as if it were the day she sat beside me showing me how to crochet on her sunporch.

We drove straight to the two-story Georgian brick house, Greenfields, my grandfather built and moved into just five years before he died. The handsome entry was held aloft by columns with ornately carved headers and footers, with wrought-iron railings beside the front steps, and a nearby post topped with a horse's head with a ring in its mouth. I remembered the one Christmas when all of the family gathered there. I was only about ten years old and jealous of my cousin, who received a pony tied to the post on Christmas morning.

The front windows were shuttered and had keystones above them. On the right side was the sunroom with its many-paned windows. On the left, a screened-in porch where Mamaw was served breakfast every morning under a whirring fan. Sadly, like the crumbling circular driveway, there were signs everywhere of benign neglect, and not so benign. The porte cochere at the back of the house had been removed. The only evidence of Mamaw's formal garden was the dry, concrete fish pond. Along the back of the house there had been a dirt road with enough shotgun houses to accommodate fifteen black families. Now, there was no sign of the community who worked Ashland Plantation.

Since no one was home, we couldn't ask to see the interior. It was almost too much to bear, staring at a grand old lady in decline. Perhaps I was just beginning to take in a side of my grandmother that I never expected to see. Before we left, we walked to the front yard, a good five hundred yards deep, and stared up into the giant magnolia tree that we climbed a hundred times as children. Looking out at the lawn, I recalled an article I kept and filed many years ago. It was written by Paul Flowers for the *Commercial Appeal* in Memphis and was published on July 7, 1948. The subject was Mamaw's fish fry, held annually for the field hands. In the pecan groves at the old homesite, Mamaw prepared a hot meal, ice cream, games, and camaraderie for more than two hundred men, women, and children whose families had worked the land for five generations. This year, not so long after her son may have killed two men, was just a repeat of a long tradition which Flowers saw coming to an end. He wrote:

> One of these days, maybe there won't be any more of those July fish frys at the Fields place in Sharkey County for a new age is coming to this Delta. The roar of the tractor is replacing the bray of the mule, and lots of folks have been moving away to town. Now so many fields are tilled by people who come out in the morning in trucks, and go back to town at night in those same trucks, and many tenant houses stand vacant. Maybe they never will be occupied again. Maybe some day there won't be any 200 souls on the Fields places and no fish frys, and the third and fourth generations of Fields won't know the names of all their folks, and the tradition will be gone. Something will be missing, and maybe what comes will be better, but there won't be that reciprocal feeling of good will between employer and employee. There may be signed contracts and formal relationships, but when

those things come, the boss is not going to be worrying about medicine for sick babies, nor about comfort for people too old to work. Or July fish frys.

The old order is passing. Only now and then appears something like this gesture in the grove at Anguilla. After all, lifetime associations have a meaning, and human affections are real.

I have no doubt that my grandmother held those fish frys with the best of intentions. It probably didn't hurt relations with black workers. Maybe she hoped to slow down the passing of the old order, but the racial system at that time was brittle and it fractured under the pressure of small, incremental changes.

These very workers on the lawn at Greenfields lived beneath the white pretense of aristocracy and moral duplicity. They had no legal protection and only two options for changing their lives: suppress their anger and stay, or leave the Delta for good. Migration to cities like Chicago, St. Louis, and Detroit was already happening. But if they stayed, they had to accept the Delta tolerance for a white man's sexual use of a black woman, the taboo of eating at the same table with a white person, the requirement that they only call at the back door of a white residence, the brutality of certain bosses, the indifference of many planters and their families.

⚶

Jay and I got in the car and drove over by Deer Creek to the Methodist church where Mamaw's funeral was conducted in 1984. From there, we headed out to the Golden Link Cemetery. Several acres away stood a copse of ancient oak trees dripping with Spanish moss, where a group of about a dozen black men stood on the day Mamaw's body was interred. I will never forget the otherworldly sound of their voices raised in respect for "Ole Miss," as they called her. The dirge they sang was deep and dark, immensely sad, and beautiful at the same time.

Jay lingered, reading the oldest tombstones even as a cloud-burst drenched us both. I got in the car and thought about how I felt at home on this flat land and, somehow, more whole for having visited these places again as a much older, single, and independent woman.

"Jay, I feel like I'm seeing this place for the first time, even though it feels more like home than any place else. I think it's because the fog we've walked around in for most of our lives is gone now."

"I know what you mean exactly. Something is ending right here, right now."

We left for Greenville, tired and coated with Delta dust. Jay said that we'd done all we could do, there was no need to spend any more time. We could head for Asheville in the morning. "There isn't anything we have learned that changes the fact that Dad acted in self-defense."

I wasn't so sure. "We've come an awfully long way, Jay. *Damn it.* I'm not ready to leave. Can we sleep on things and make a decision in the morning?" He agreed, so we drove north to a small dive in downtown Greenville. The wine wasn't rotgut but it tasted pretty tannic. There was a trio playing the blues. That was nice. We ate fried seafood on the mushy side.

The next morning, I dredged up enough courage to place a phone call to my uncle Bill's widow who lived in Jackson. She and Aunt Sis were the only surviving relatives of Dad's generation.

"Aunt Lib, how are you? Jay and I are in Greenville. We've been doing some research here." I told her about how seedy the downtown area was.

She seemed wary of asking what we were looking into. "Oh yes, when your uncle Bill and I lived in the Delta, I did a lot of our shopping in Greenville. There were several really good shops. It just breaks my heart to go there now." Aunt Lib, still stately and pretty, sewed most of her four daughters' clothes when they were young. As Uncle Bill became more successful with cotton farming, she enjoyed decorating her home with antiques and reproductions from places like Winterthur in Delaware.

Then I asked her if she remembered the shooting.

"No, I was not married to Uncle Bill in 1946. I was a coed at Ole Miss, a freshman. But I tell you what, Molly, I would just let this die a quiet death. Who have you talked to about it?"

I answered her question partially and then asked if Jay and I might drop by for a visit before driving back to Asheville, but without any specific excuse, she declined.

"My suggestion to you would be that you don't stir up this thing about your daddy. Let sleeping dogs lie."

When I told Jay about the conversation, I sensed that he took Lib's lack of hospitality and fierce refusal to talk as indications that we were on unsafe ground. He didn't have much to say about the shooting after that. Part of him seemed to go to another place.

☙❦❧

Our trip ended after a second visit to the courthouse in Rolling Fork. Upstairs, in the attic, we found bound issues of the *Pilot* even older than the ones we perused the day before. Pat pulled on a pair of yellow latex gloves and took us into a small, octagonal room that was full of paper and full of dust. There were boxes and stacks of old docket books, so many that all of us couldn't fit in the room. With some luck, Jay was able to locate the two years we missed the day before at the newspaper office. I stood outside in the hall with a gathering sense of frustration. My inclination was to go through all of the boxes and books, every last one, if it took us all day and even the next. I felt like we were not being thorough enough. What I didn't understand then was that there would not be one source, one map of what happened. Instead, I would have to pick up crumbs on the forest path—one at a time. Since we were not free to rummage, we took the two years of *Pilot*s downstairs.

In the September 3, 1948, issue, I found an editorial Dad wrote in response to a series of articles published in the Pittsburgh newspaper by a journalist, Ray Sprigle, who disguised himself as a

"Negro," planted himself in the Deep South, and then wrote about his experience. It must have really galled Dad that this man's "false" impressions would become the adopted view of many in the Northeast.

He countered: "The South is the American home of the Negro race. They were brought here out of the jungles of Africa. The unfortunate part of a Sprigle-like action is the consequence borne on the men and women of both races who are working toward an ever approaching goal of progress for both races with progress for the Negro race ranking first in their minds because of extreme need . . ." The editorial went on with a vengeance and when I finished reading it, I turned to Jay and said, "This is what you might call 'enlightened racism.'" Dad and Mamaw had shown us again and again that they loved and respected and cared for the black workers in the only way that they knew how. They wanted "the best" for them, unless that meant giving up power. Maybe when Dad wrote this, he was ready to surrender a bit. Maybe his actions in 1946 had cost him. It was only five months after he wrote this editorial that he moved our family to Tennessee. I think he knew he would never again live in the Mississippi Delta. I think he was looking for the cure that would make his incessant headache go away. Already he had tucked the memory of the December 12 incident into some distant compartment of his brain.

᮪

Just as we opened the door to leave, I turned to Pat. "Can I run through our process with you just in case we have overlooked something that you might think of? Any person we might need to talk to?"

She listened. Then paused. "Actually, it might be a good idea for you to call Merlin Richardson, over in Anguilla. He's the mayor and has held that office for many years. I'll get his phone number for you."

CHAPTER SIX

What King Evans Told Me

May 2006

I could hardly wait to get back to Asheville so I could call the mayor
from the quiet of my home. But driving the 650 miles across the
South with Jay was not going to be quick or direct. Only an hour
out of Anguilla, he wanted to stop in Yazoo City to visit the Willie
Morris exhibit at the local museum. I remembered one of Dad's
typed reminiscences. He posted it to Laura, Jay, and me.

> The following is occasioned by a Christmas 1990 gift from
> my son, Jay Fields, Jr., of *Faulkner's Mississippi*, with text
> by Willie Morris, who grew up in Yazoo City, whose Yazoo
> County adjoins our native Sharkey County, Mississippi, and
> with haunting photographs by William Eggleston, the Mem-
> phis photographer.
>
> I met William Faulkner on two occasions.
> Neither of these meetings were significant in the context
> of voluminous bibliography and the even more pervasive
> folk tales which have proliferated apace the author's growing
> greatness. I record them simply because they occurred and
> are doomed to expire with me if I do not do so.
>
> Meeting One: Early winter of 1949.
> I had returned from my boarding house lunch to my desk
> as owner/editor of Rolling Fork, Mississippi's *The Deer Creek
> Pilot*. Jack Dayle Shults, a free-lance photographer on whom

I relied for the small amount of photography my anemic weekly consumed, sauntered in with:

"Guess who's in town?"

I didn't bother with guessing and went straight to:

"Who?"

"William Faulkner," Jack answered.

"Where is he?" I continued.

"Well, he got a haircut and shave at Roney's Barber Shop and is just finishing lunch at the Courthouse Café. He came in with some fellows been deer hunting out of a camp in the national forest."

"Got your camera with you?" I asked.

"No, but I can get it real fast," Jack said, heading for the door.

Within minutes, Jack was back and [we] sauntered across the block to the café. Faulkner had finished his lunch and stood alone on a nearby corner, readily recognizable because of the many pictures of him that had been occasioned by the filming in Lafayette County of *Intruder in the Dust*.

I was immediately struck by a memory of my father who had died some 14 years earlier when I was 13. Both men were small of stature. Both men were of neat appearance. Faulkner's hair was trimmed and his face ruddy from the application of the barber's hot towels and generous palmsful of bay rum.

"Mr. Faulkner, I'm H. J. Fields, editor of our local weekly newspaper. Do you mind if we get a photograph of you here in Rolling Fork?" I asked hesitantly.

"Not at all," he answered, removing a toothpick from the center of his mouth but otherwise not particularly posing, except to lift his head toward the camera lens. I stepped out of the area of focus and watched as Jack performed every photographer's rite of coaching his subject and asking for just one more. On conclusion of the picture-taking, I reapproached Faulkner, extending my hand.

"Thank you so much, Mr. Faulkner. It's an honor to have you in our town," I said.

"Well, thank you," Faulkner replied, shifting his toothpick from right to left hand and giving my hand a solid shake.

At that time I didn't know much about newspapering and had no remote idea about interviewing—especially interviewing a celebrity.

So, for a few minutes longer, I engaged Faulkner in small talk relative to the success (or lack of it) of his hunt. Memory dims and I will not attempt to dignify that mostly one-sided conversation with quotations.

After a while, I thanked Faulkner a final time and Jack and I left for the newspaper office.

We left him standing in the exact spot we'd found him, solitary, at ease.

Dad's second encounter with Faulkner occurred on Derby Day, 1951, at Churchill Downs. My grandfather Fleming offered Dad a seat on his annual chartered flight to Louisville. From Dad's description of this event, I could tell that his enthusiasm for going had little to do with horses. He entered the scene as a young journalist, taking in the colorful and elegant social atmosphere, reveling in camaraderie, legitimized gambling, and the sweet taste of mint juleps. Though he planned to write up this event in the press box where the other newspapermen would be hanging out and then wire it from there, he left home without press credentials, so between races, he had to go to the telegraph office. Upon returning to his seat in the grandstands, Dad spied Faulkner engaged in conversation with two impassive gatekeepers.

Dad recognized him immediately, walked up, introduced himself, and offered to help. He escorted the renowned author to the office of the director of public relations, Bill Corum, and sent word to him via his secretary that Faulkner was there. Then he returned to his seat, proud and happy to have brushed up against the great Mississippian again.

Dad's experiences and his love of good writing made a deep impression on me. I thought about how he might have become one of Mississippi's best if he hadn't been riven in two. As long as he lived in the Delta with Mom, he would straddle the line between the legacy of his forebears and the germinating changes in the landscape and the culture.

My father, the writer, was proud of his profession, happy with his associates in it, and respectful of the power of words. He had the sensibilities of a writer. He pondered things long and hard. He read widely the fiction of his day. He was smart, perceptive, and creative. These traits did not square up, in my mind, with a person capable of murder.

❦

Back on the road, Jay must have sensed my fatigue and sorrow and, typical of him, suggested that we would be foolish not to drive upstate to Oxford. He knew I was reluctant to let a good bookstore pass me by. Once there, we walked the city plaza and stopped in at Square Books for an hour of perusing. Then, it wouldn't do to leave without a cold beer and barbeque at one of the Ole Miss hangouts.

From there we drove east to the Natchez Trace.

I asked Jay, "Did you, Dad, and Julia [Dad's second wife] drive down this road to Mamaw's funeral in '85?"

"No, we took the Memphis route. How 'bout you?"

"We drove down with Laura and Scott. I was behind the wheel and caught up in conversation. Forgot the speed limit on the Trace was fifty-five. We were barreling south toward Anguilla when I saw a flashing light in the oncoming lane. But I didn't know that troopers would or even could clock a driver in the opposite lane. I slowed down to be safe, and sure enough, he was after me.

"I really got scared when he got out of his car and stood . . . oh, six plus feet tall. He was black. I hadn't ever seen a black trooper and it was kinda scary."

"What happened?"

"I think he must have sensed my fear. He smiled and asked to see my license.

"'Miss Walling, did you know you were speeding?'

"I told him no and apologized. Told him we were going to our grandmother's funeral. He looked at me from behind his shaded eyes and said, 'I'll let you off but don't let there be a next time.'"

Jay said, "Maybe he had a favorite grandmother too."

⚭

Back in Asheville, I felt wonderful to be in my safe and cozy home. I found the scrap of paper Pat Thrasher gave me with Mayor Richardson's phone number on it. Before the day was out, I called his house. He was eager to talk to me since he knew my family and worked in the cotton business for forty years. But he did not recollect the shooting in 1946.

Then, "Wait a minute. I do know a ninety-three-year-old black man named King Evans. He has lived in Anguilla practically all his life and he might know what you are talking about. Let me see if I can find him and I'll get right back to you."

The empty fridge could wait a few hours. I did some of those chores women do when they have things on their minds . . . sorted dirty clothes, made lists, watered the houseplants, opened the mail.

Around 4:00 the phone rang.

Age may have eaten away at the voice of Mr. Evans, but it had not affected his mental acuity.

"Oh yes, I remember. Your daddy was going to clean up Anguilla. There was a service station, a Pan Am station, where black women were picked up by white men and they sold illegal alcohol there. Your daddy went to the customers instead of the proprietor. His objective of getting the folks off the street and out of town could have been achieved by asking the proprietor to close for the night. The customers would have moved out of town and this incident could have possibly been avoided in my opinion. Jesse [that's what he called my dad] was hit by David Jones. And then, when your daddy saw David reach for his .45 Colt, he fired on him.

"I was coming back into town about that time, from working in the fields, and I saw Simon Toombs on the ground. Your daddy thought he could just tell the customers to go home. This is an example of 'absolute power corrupting absolutely.' Do you know what I mean?"

I said I did, but it took me a minute to get the gist—probably some form of denial on my part. I knew that whites in the South held absolute dominion over blacks. I just didn't want to go to the place in my mind that informed me of possibilities of corruption.

"My uncle Tom was wounded in the shooting. He was shot in the shoulder," I said.

"I don't recall that. I don't recall that at all. Dr. Crawford was sheriff. Your grandmother cried so hard that he agreed to take your daddy to his home rather than put him in the jail like a common criminal."

He told me that Uncle Bill was the first landowner to sell acreage to blacks so that they could own land of their own. Maybe that was an effort to make restitution.

Then Mr. Evans asked if I would like to read his book, *Backroads of My Memory*, which he said contained his thoughts on growing up black in the South. I sent for it right away and read it through in one sitting. So intrigued by what he had written and how it fit into the scheme of my father's life, I called Mr. Evans and asked if he would be willing to talk with me in person. Less than a week later I got a call from his daughter, Carolyn Hackett. We made a date for July 16. I would make the second trip to Mississippi alone.

❦

My mind didn't rest for the next two months. It was busy sorting through the maelstrom of facts and suppositions, slotting details into coherent order. I was putting together a cogent picture, as accurately as I could. But I needed to start again . . . with family history and historical context.

෧෦෨

Land was at the heart of the tragedy: black alluvial, buckshot, and sandy loam soil in the Mississippi Delta where we grew some of the finest long-staple cotton in America. When my great-grandfather returned to Sharkey County after his stint in the Civil War, he returned to poverty and the broken-down industries of the defeated South. The wealth potential of the land was dependent on a large supply of black labor. In 1850, the ratio of black to white in Washington County, Mississippi, was 14.5 to 1. Now, with the abolition of slavery, financial and social success was compromised. Harris Jesse found a room in a boardinghouse, and every day washed his coveralls and left them out on the line to dry at night. Someone stole them one dark evening, so he went to work in his long johns until he could afford to buy new ones. In *Memoirs of Mississippi*, a book I found in the Rolling Fork Library, Harris is characterized: "He commenced planting on a part of the plantation of which he is now owner and where he laid the foundations of his present success, by hard work, close attention to business and by denying himself many of the conveniences and luxuries which the young men of the present day think indispensable to their welfare and happiness." One year later, on December 26, 1866, he married Martha Katharine Sullivan, a native of Issaquena County and daughter of John Sullivan. She was purported to have been heir to her father's fortune. The first five children they produced died in infancy, probably from malaria. In the pre-levee days, the swampy areas of the county kept the mosquitoes busy, and sometimes water stood under houses for long periods of time. Yellow fever also took the lives of many slaves.

Harris and Martha didn't give up on having children, and in the end there were thirteen births. In 1880, Harris rented the

eight-hundred-acre Woolfolk Plantation, which he soon purchased for forty thousand dollars, and paid off in five years. At
the height of his success, my great-grandfather had amassed three
thousand acres, had a half interest in the cottonseed oil works,
and was a major stockholder in the Bank of Anguilla, which he
and Mr. Bernard Pearl started.

Before he died, Harris Jesse meted out his substantial land
holdings to his sons and daughters. Thomas, my grandfather,
came into possession of the 572 acres that comprised Ashland
Plantation. Dad's parents stayed in the house at Ashland until
the last of their four offspring was born. Then, in 1931, Tom built
Greenfields, the two-story brick, Georgian-style house on Highway 61, not five miles from Ashland. He and my grandmother
moved the four children into their new home. It sat back from
the highway some thousand feet and had a circular driveway
that split so that cars could park in front or in back of the house.
An alley ran the width of the property. Some of the women
who lived on the place helped to staff the house. Aunt Mat was
enlisted to help Mamaw raise the kids after Granddaddy died.
Neither she nor Josephine, or "Jo," who cleaned house, fit the
image of the "mammy" as mythologized by southerners whose
goal it was to dispel any notion that black women were unhappy,
or that they were attractive to white men, or that they weren't
devoted to their mistress and her children. The men worked the
fields, kept up the yard, and helped out at the gin during harvest.
Servants on the plantation worked long, hard hours, day in and
day out. One planter's wife described her servant's workday thus:
"Mary's first chore was milking fourteen cows. She then cooked
breakfast, swept the house, made the beds, dusted, washed the
dishes, prepared meals for some of the other servants, nursed
her own infant, and at last, ate breakfast. Immediately thereafter,
she cleaned the kitchen, prepared a huge midday meal, washed
dishes, cleaned the dining room, washed a large batch of clothes
and hung them out, and began preparing supper. After supper
she milked for a second time that day, nursed her child, cleaned
the kitchen, and retired."

Highway 61 wound through Anguilla's "downtown," a tiny grid of streets with no particular pattern. The main sources of commerce were the Bank of Anguilla, the Gibbs Store, the barbershop, and a drugstore. There was a Chinese grocery that necessitated a special school for immigrants and other nonwhites. Reconstruction had made it difficult to secure labor. At first planters were eager to try immigrants in the fields but became discouraged because they were far less willing to be cooperative than the blacks were. The small town also boasted an oil mill, three cotton gins, a post office, city hall, a three-story brick schoolhouse, and a depot for the train that ran from Memphis to New Orleans and back. Since Anguilla was situated on Deer Creek, with the Sunflower River nearby, flooding was an ongoing concern. After the great flood of 1927, levees were built and proper drainage kept the town safe and dry. Three service stations provided gas for farm equipment and autos.

In 1946, the town claimed 500 residents—the entire county had a population of 15,433 and was 70 percent black. When Dad and his two brothers, Tom and Bill, returned home from the war, they found that life, as they had known it, had begun to change. The homesickness Dad had expressed in his letter to family from Africa was engendered by an idealized picture of home that helped to sustain him while he was under the stress of war in a distant country. Once he returned to Anguilla, his image of a perfect home didn't fit the reality anymore.

I wanted to understand why tension in such a small town could reach a flash point that resulted in the death of two men. First I turned to the book *The Mind of the South,* published in 1941. It helped me to see the social dynamic at work on most plantations. "[T]he plantation tended to find its center in itself: to be an independent social unit, a self-contained and largely self-sufficient little world of its own." The author, W. J. Cash, viewed that world as akin to frontier life where individualism was prized and the will of the landowner would represent the law. "[T]hat the individualism of the plantation world would be one which, like that of the backcountry before it, would be far too much concerned with balk, immediate, unsupported assertion of the ego, which placed too great stress on the inviolability of personal whim . . . and the boast, voiced or not, on the part of every Southerner that he would knock hell out of whoever dared to cross him." To get more to the point of the conflict that occurred in the "coloreds only" room at the Pan Am station, the changes resulting from black men's service in the military were perhaps uppermost in Dad's and his brothers' minds.

❧

Dad came home from the war, decided to go into newspaper work, and focused his attention on local issues and the changing South. Out of necessity, Bill and Tom took up farming, and they were seeing the results of dissension in the field hands. Sometimes, they didn't show up for work and that resulted in 250 pounds of unpicked cotton per person, per day. As managers, they would have to go to Jackson or Greenville to hire immigrants to do the work. They thought ready access to alcohol had eroded the work ethic.

Dad's editorials appeared under the column head "The Pilot House" and he wrote about these concerns. He lamented the loss of the old order, complained that now "white-trash" service station owners were selling alcohol to coloreds. This situation led to rowdy behavior and aggression, but it was fruitless to expect "the law" to handle the situation. In one lengthy editorial, following a successful vote to extend prohibition, Dad wrote, "You can't dry up a flood with a pocket handkerchief and Sherriff Crawford can't stop the liquor being sold in the County. The Sherriff's office is run on your tax money; the bootleggers operate on the profit they make from selling whisky. They can, and do, match $100 in avoiding the law to every $1 he has to applying the law to them." This was one of numerous editorials on the subject of alcohol written to wake up the public. It's fair to say that the slow progress of change in this arena was frustrating the hell out of my father.

CHAPTER SEVEN

Big

May 2006

Before venturing back to Mississippi, I vacillated between thinking about Dad the writer and Dad the gunslinger. One thing was for certain: he was bigger than life. In fact, my mother quietly gave Dad the nickname "Big," and used it when he was out of earshot. I doubt she knew that Dad weighed eleven pounds when he was born or that he was allowed to breast feed until he was four. Before she died, Mamaw told me that he was walking and talking when he quit. I still shudder at that thought.

As a younger man, he developed a larger vision of life and its possibilities, I think, as a result of his education at Davidson College, his experiences in the war, his avid consumption of good books and his contemplative nature. After all, he'd spent the idle hours of his boyhood reading *Boy's Life*, *American Boy*, and his favorite newspaper, the Sunday *New York Times*, which his father subscribed to and which arrived with five- day-old news.

I thought about the time he gave me a signed copy of Eudora Welty's "Music from Spain." It was copy number 164 of the 775 that were printed. He was so inspired by it that he went home and wrote an editorial about the Levee Press. He saw it as a significant cultural event that Hodding Carter and Ben Wasson, literary agent and critic, had aspired to capture and elevate the status of Mississippi writers by opening the press.

Dad wrote, "More distressing is the fact that southern literary works are graded on a basis of will-it-be-interesting—in New

England, by editors and publishers with eastern and northern tastes and standards.

"In developing the South industrially, agriculturally, and economically, we must not fail to see that cultural developments go hand in hand with the more material gains.

"The Levee Press, and efforts of its nature, is helping to keep the balance."

৹৻৹

In 1948, two years after the shootings, the *Deer Creek Pilot* was awarded Best Weekly of the Year for papers under twenty-five hundred circulation by the Mississippi Press Association. One issue I read covered a wide spectrum of news: "This Week in Washington," the war with Russia, proceedings of the board of supervisors, the school board, an editorial promoting the Red Cross—"Farmers deserve help," legal notices, personals, garden club news, Dale Carnegie, John Deere and Coke ads, classified, and an ad for the Joy Theatre in Rolling Fork, showing Betty Grable in *Mother Wore Tights*. One of Dad's articles wound up in the Seattle *Post Intelligencer*. He had made a good decision to follow his heart into newspaper work. But other questions were coming to me. How did he walk about in public with his head held high after killing two men without consequence? In a later conversation with my mother, she told me that Dad never mentioned the incident after he came home from being incarcerated. He didn't appear to be fearful. She didn't know what he thought about it. At this early stage in my discovery process, I found this hard to imagine. For Dad to walk away and feel nothing was unconscionable to me, but like my mother, I just "didn't understand it."

৹৻৹

In the late 1940s, before Dad decided to leave the Delta, he was offered a job at another newspaper. Somehow he caught the attention of the person doing the hiring at the *New York Times*. Because Dad had a resume that included such diverse roles at the *Deer Creek Pilot* as publisher, editor, advertising manager, pressman, printer, linotype machine operator, and reporter, it was thought that he would bring a unique perspective to a writing position on the staff. According to my brother, "I would have to believe that the offer would have been largely based on samples of his writing which, of course, were excellent." When we asked Dad why he decided not to accept the job, he always said that it would have been too hard to move his young family to New York.

My mother says she doesn't remember this. Since she herself lived in New York during the war years, she would have had valuable input into the decision. After Uncle Joe died in India in the war, Mom drove to Delray Beach, Florida, to console her parents. Their grief was almost more than they could bear and so it was for Mom too, but my grandparents had an abundance of friends who wintered in Florida. They frequently entertained. One evening Mom was introduced to Frank White, vice president for CBS in the New York office. While having cocktails in the garden, he told Mom, "If at any time you want a job, I'll give you one. I think you should make a break." To her utter disbelief, Mam and Joe encouraged her to go to New York.

Shortly thereafter, Mom was invited to share an apartment with three young women from Bristol. They lived at 116th Street at Riverside Drive near Columbia University. Mom's share of the rent was twenty-five dollars a month and each one put three dollars in a kitty for groceries. When she stepped off the train with her suitcases, nineteen years old, she said, "Jesus, this is a big place for me to be." Once settled, she started her office job at CBS. Mom was in charge of making TV assignments. She lived close enough to Liederkranz Hall to walk. Arthur Godfrey, George Burns, and Gracie Allen were on the program every day. She heard Jan Peerce and Lily Pons. On one occasion, she walked to Broadway to hear Frank Sinatra perform at the Paramount Theatre. In addition to her "ideal" job and the nightlife of the city, Mom and her apartment mates enjoyed dating the boys who were going overseas for the war. They were frequently taken out to dinner and the movies. Life was better than she ever imagined it could be.

Would Mom have encouraged Dad to take the job in New York? We can't know. Her experience there would probably have created a positive response to the possibility, especially since she despised living in the Delta. But to enter, again, the environment she had known as a young, single woman may have seemed daunting to a mother of two very small children.

☙❧

I wrote a letter to King Evans asking for clarification on several points, one being the issue of Dad's safety after the killings. He responded in this way: "No, I don't believe your father would have had reason to be fearful. Very few, if any, whites were killed in retribution for acts of violence against blacks. Under the Jim Crow system blacks were powerless to retaliate against whites. This was especially true in areas as the South Delta where our entire livelihood depended on the white landowner. However, some whites were killed in moments of anger or robbery. In most instances blacks would leave the area, some never to return, to avoid harm if they had altercations or incidents with whites. Black families were destroyed when this occurred and some have never been reunited if they left on the run."

In early spring 1949, soon after I was born, Dad made the decision to move our family to east Tennessee. He gave the following reasons for leaving Mississippi: "I returned from military service to the Delta and remained for five years before absenting myself permanently. The post-Raj days had ended, tractors had replaced the mule power of my father's day, relations between blacks and whites had taken on new dimensions and the Delta had become stories for more gifted writers and more accurate historians." While his words reveal an intellectually sophisticated grip on what was happening in the Delta, why couldn't he live with those changes? What if black/white relations had taken on dimensions of accountability and retribution?

ঔ৹

After we resettled in Knoxville, I saw another side of Dad. An incident occurred when I was six years old, after the dynamics in our home had changed with Dad's late afternoon toddies becoming an everyday thing. His mood darkened and Mom became unhappy and tense. I started to react physically to the stress and developed skin rashes that spread from my arms to my scalp and parts in between. I had a serious bout of mononucleosis. Mom forced me to take lengthy naps that I hated and that made me bored and restless.

One afternoon, I sat on the window seat in my room, turning pages in story books. It was summertime so the windows were open, curtains flapping in the breeze. The sound of a distant cry of distress caught my attention. I listened harder. Across Kingston Pike from our house several acres of pastureland lay undisturbed and covered in tall yellow grass. I looked out my window but could see nothing except a tractor in the field, but the cries continued until I covered my ears to keep from hearing them. Finally, I ventured downstairs to the kitchen where our black maid, Sarah, was ironing and Mom was puttering about.

"Mama, I hear someone yelling over there, across the highway."

"It's probably a cat. Go back upstairs and don't come down until I tell you to."

Back in my room, I tried to ignore the cries but at last I resolved that there was no cat at fault. Down to the kitchen I went, sheepishly, two more times.

With fear of bodily harm, I entered the kitchen again. Sarah looked up from her ironing board at me and raised her eyebrows as if to say, "Chil', you askin' for it."

Mom swung round when she realized I was there.

"All right, young lady, we are going outside, and I'll show you that you are wrong."

We walked out the front door and down the sidewalk. Mom stood still, listened, became tense, and I felt her hand tighten around mine. "I need to call your father and an ambulance. Go back upstairs and wait in your room."

Just before we sat down to supper that night, Dad limped in the back door. His tee shirt was stained with red clay, his khaki pants were ripped up one side, and when he pulled up the torn, bloody, pant leg, it exposed a deep scrape that ran from his ankle to his knee. Blue bruising and angry red swollen tissue ran along his shinbone. He was exhausted but sat down with Jay and me and told us what had happened, that the man who owned that field was trying to mow. He couldn't see the deep gully in front of him because of tall grass. His tractor tipped over, and he fell off and under it. He was pinned there for hours. His leg was badly broken. He was weak and his voice was worn out from yelling. They took him to the hospital.

I looked at my father with a whole new appreciation after he was injured while offering assistance across the highway. He was taller, stronger, big-hearted, and heroic.

❧

From 1951 to 1955, Dad worked for the *Knoxville News Sentinel* as utility copy editor and state editor. If he covered news stories, he didn't have a byline, so when I looked through the microfilm for signs of Dad, I found only a few feature articles that he wrote when the regular columnist was away from his desk. Each one had a half-column-by-one-inch caricature of Dad—wearing a bow tie. One article had sport cars as its subject. Dad loved automobiles of every stripe. He bought one of the first subcompacts on the market, a baby-blue VW bug. On weekends, he and Mom loaded us three kids and a picnic in the small interior space, and off we drove to the Smoky Mountains outside Knoxville where we had a favorite "watering hole" for swimming and rock-skipping contests.

Another article featured a story about a fractious fisherman. Dad reflected on how he would rather wear a straitjacket than get so caught up in a sport capable of frustrating a grown man to the point of insanity.

And a third article was written from Delray Beach where Dad was vacationing with the family, running back and forth between his mother's cottage and Mam and Joe's. He reminisces about his marriage to my mother on the patio outside his window. Then he does a crafty job of running down a list of reasons why a person would want to spend a winter month in Florida, but we find out in the end that he wasn't able to partake of the pleasures of golfing, dog racing, or eating pompano because he contracted the mumps from me.

I do not recall my father making any overt racial statements during those growing-up years in Knoxville. My family kept a black housekeeper in its employ for as long as I can remember, but Dad never treated her with disdain or disrespect.

Up until the May 17, 1954, issue of the *Sentinel*, there is little coverage of any racial dissension—of anything racial at all. Though there had been flash fires over segregation in the schools since the mid-nineteenth century, no one on the staff of the paper at that time was inclined to report it. But on the day the Supreme Court ruled segregation unconstitutional, the front page headline for the United Press release read: "Separate, but Equal Doctrine Ruled Out." Chief Justice Warren said, "To separate them [black children] from others of similar age and qualifications solely because of their race generates a feeling of inferiority as to their status in the community that may affect their hearts and minds in a way unlikely ever to be undone." Pictured on the op-ed page are George Hayes of Washington, Thurgood Marshall, special counsel for the NAACP, and James Nebrit, professor at Howard University who argued the case.

I'm sure my father read every word of these articles, including the reference to the case as the most important since the Dred

Scott decision of 1857 that held that a Negro was not a citizen. He would have made special note of the fact that the Democratic representative from Mississippi called this new court decision a " 'tragic ruling' but not too surprising in view of the caliber of men on the court."

Another article in this issue featured Negro teachers as the biggest problem in Knoxville. At that time, the county employed only 12 black teachers out of 729 in the school system. The possibility that a black teacher might find herself teaching a class composed of predominantly white students was high. This fact would have been difficult for Dad to stomach since Jay and I were both attending public elementary school.

I have only one childhood memory of Dad in an incident involving a black person. It was Christmastime and one of our family traditions was to spend an evening downtown at Rich's in the toy department. First, Mom and Dad carted us out to dinner at the S & W Cafeteria and asked us what we wanted Santa to bring that year. In those days, there were few advertisements in the press or on TV displaying the new crop of toys. We had to make our wish list on the spot as we toured the shelves at Rich's. After oohing and aahing over the Poor Pitiful Pearl doll, Silly Putty, books, and games, I was sent down the aisles to the long hall where a bank of elevators off-loaded shoppers on that floor. Shadow boxed displays of Christmas scenes lined the walls and provided ample entertainment while parents made their selections. While I was caught up in a wintery dreamscape, the elevator doors opened and a young black boy, maybe three or four years older than I was, stepped off and walked up beside me.

"Look at that fancy Christmas tree," he might have said. I nodded and pretended he wasn't standing so close to my side.

"Wanta give me a kiss?" he asked. This time I shook my head "no" and started to walk away in the direction of my parents but they were out of view, so I went down the first aisle of toys.

"Aw, c'mon, give me a kiss."

This time I answered, "No" and broke into a run. Still no sign of Mom or Dad.

He became more insistent and put his hand on my shoulder to turn me in his direction. I shrugged him off and picked up my pace.

"Don't be shy, now. Just one kiss is all I want."

About that time, I spied my dad, who was intently watching this transaction.

"Molly, come here," he said, his face turning crimson, and when the boy heard the anger in Dad's voice, he turned away. Just as fast, Dad had him by the scruff of his neck.

"Where the hell do you think you are going?" Dad asked and just as quickly as he could, commandeered the kisser into the hands of the floor manager. "I want him thrown out of this store." And his demand was met forthwith. I started to shake and clung to my parents' sides until our shopping venture was over. Somehow I knew that a kiss from a black boy was a stigma I could not afford. That sentiment had come to me directly from my father, but this incident was not an example of his racist tendencies. I believe he would have handled a young white boy the same way.

Jay related a story of his own stint working at the *News Sentinel*. He was finishing his undergraduate degree in journalism at UT and completing a practicum as copyboy. He said, "I'd pull content flowing in across the wire machines, UPI, AP, Reuters, and the *New York Times*. Then I'd separate out into sports, international, national, regional, and local news and drop off the individual pieces on relevant desks around the newsroom. I think I worked there for about three months. The managing editor was there when Dad was state editor in the fifties. He knew Dad's "Old South" predilections, so, when I came in for the copyboy job, he pulled me to the side and made reference to the fact that I would be working for a black copyboy staff chief and asked me if I had any objection to that since he figured Dad might have a bias against it. I was kind of surprised but appreciated the gesture in a kind of left-handed way. I actually really, really liked the black fellow, not much older than I was, who was very graceful and nice and professional in what he did. I was actually very pleased he was my boss."

༺༻

One day in Knoxville stamped itself into my memory in technicolor. I was nine years old and the year was 1958. After Dad left his desk at the *News Sentinel* and drove into the driveway each evening around 5:30, I put down my bike and raced to his side for a welcome home hug. Then he changed into khakis and a tee shirt. His shiny dogtag hung around his neck and even though he had been out of the military over ten years, he still carried a toned physique with pride. He tanned easily, and when he smiled, his cheeks plumped up and a square jaw protruded.

He always poured himself an old-fashioned glass full of scotch and water and called to us kids, "Molly, Jay, Laura. Let's go down in the pasture and watch for the big trucks on Kingston Pike." My little sister's arrival in '54 had necessitated our family's move to a bigger house near the construction site of Interstate 40.

We did this "truck thing" almost every night. We scurried after Dad, plopped down in the tall grass, and waited. When the semis went past our spot, we jumped up, crooked our arms, and tugged on invisible fan cords in the sky. Occasionally, the drivers caught sight of us and blew their horns.

"He saw *me* that time, Molly," Jay yelled.

"Uh-huh."

As the day faded to dusk, if Mom hadn't called us to dinner, Dad settled us down to listen to his stories. Sometimes they had to do with his boyhood in Mississippi. Sometimes they were regular fairy tales. In love with the Bible stories I learned at the Methodist church but still unsure, I asked, "Daddy, how do you know there is a God?"

"Well, let's say we are camping at our swimming hole over in the mountains. And let's say that your mother and I have left you and Jay at the campsite while we take a short hike. While you're playing, a big, angry, black bear ambles out of the woods and comes toward our tents. You and Jay think that the bear might gobble you up. You freeze in fear. Here's where God comes in. Close by there are other campers who have just put a big steak on their campfire. Just when the bear starts to come toward you, God sends a breeze in your direction, and the bear, who is very hungry, catches the scent of the steak. Instead of coming for you, he turns in the direction of the campfire. About that time your mother and I return from our hike. We are all safe together. And nobody gets hurt. That is how God works."

I took a deep breath and felt warmth and security settle into my body. I thought that God might save me from any harm that came my way.

One particular evening after Dad came in late from the news-paper, Mom asked me to set the round oak dinner table for sup-per. That was my regular job. While I was setting out the plates, Jay, or "Bugs," as we had nicknamed him because of his promi-nent two front teeth, came in, slamming the screen door behind him. He wore his Little League jersey and pouted about Bearden Elementary School's defeat that afternoon. Now three years old, Laura came in wearing shorts, a halter top, four strands of fake pop-apart pearls, and a pair of pink, plastic high heels.

"Jay, Laura, wash your hands before dinner," Mom commanded.

The three of us sat down at the table, Laura in the middle. We waited. From out of the dark hallway, Dad entered the kitchen after changing from his suit to khaki shorts and a green golf shirt. He reached under the counter and drew out a fifth of scotch to replenish his glass. He sat down beside me and swirled the con-tents of his glass until Mom approached the table with plates of fish sticks, french-cut green beans, and steaming mashed potatoes, setting them down for Laura and me. She returned to fill three more plates. This was the same Thursday evening meal that we ate every week. It seemed that Mom only knew how to cook seven things. Almost immediately, Laura turned up the ketchup bottle and dumped three-quarters of a cup into the middle of her plate.

"By the time my mother was my age," Mom said, talking over our heads, "she had Mary and James doing her cooking and clean-ing. I need more help than one day a week."

At first, Dad ignored the comment and turned to focus on Jay's ballgame.

"Son, you don't look too happy. How'd your team do today?"

I think it was then that I began to fidget, sensing a growing frustration in Mom. I looked up at the gently swaying pull-down lamp that cast a wide beam around my family.

When Mom set Dad's plate heavily on the table with a sigh, he said, "I'm doing the best I can to provide for you and the kids. We can only afford a maid once a week. It's gonna be tight for a couple more years." He ran his knobby fingers through thick, wavy hair and peered out from under his eyebrows at my brother.

"Son, stop pushing your food around on your plate and eat it."

"We had this for lunch at school today. I'm not hungry. Can I go outside and play with Flirt and the puppies?"

"Goddamnit. You stay put and eat what your mother has cooked for you." My father's broad hand came down hard on the tabletop, causing plates and glasses to jump and rattle.

"Go ahead, Jay. You can go," Mom overruled in a hard voice, looking straight into Dad's eyes. "Aren't you even going to ask me how my day went?"

Laura, whose little face was surrounded in a halo of sweaty, blonde curls, reached for her milk and tipped the glass over. A stream of white liquid sped along the line of the table leaf and dripped onto the floor. Immediately, her face scrunched up and she forced tears out of delft blue eyes, anticipating Mom's reaction. "Oh, Lord," Mom grabbed a tea towel and went after the milk.

I watched all of this happen within the space of a few short minutes and froze in my chair, hardly breathing. Dad, seething and restless, looked over at me. His eyes traveled down my body and paused to take in the view of my legs from the hem of my shorts down. I already knew that his face was flushed enough to indicate he'd had too much to drink.

"Get up, Molly, and come with me. I'm tired of lookin' at those ugly long black hairs on your legs. I'm gonna shave 'em off."

Mom rose to her feet from the floor beside Laura's chair. "Jay, what do you think you're doing?"

He ignored her, reached down, took hold of my arm, and pulled me to my feet. Then he pointed at the stairs and said, "Go up to the bathroom."

Mom followed close behind, leaving Laura at the kitchen table. Hesitantly she said, "Jay, don't you think this can wait? She's too young." But he was unresponsive and unstoppable.

He followed me into the bathroom, lowered the Pepto-Bismol pink toilet lid that matched the tile floor, and shoved me down onto it. Through the window beside the toilet, the last rays of the sun brought light to an otherwise dark bathroom. The scent of Dad's Old Spice mixed with stale cigarette breath made me nauseous. I watched him reach into the medicine cabinet, draw out a can of Barbasol, and shake it hard. Then he reached for his Gillette razor.

Mom leaned stiffly against the doorjamb and watched with her arms crossed. She probably had on the blue and white seersucker capris and matching blouse she wore a lot then. She reached for the light switch and flipped it on. Her face was hard, lips pursed, and she watched every move Dad made. She would not look at me.

After throwing a towel on the floor beneath my feet, Dad lathered one leg while warming his razor under the spigot. His eyes appeared to bug out the way they often did when he polished his shoes on Sunday mornings before church. With an unsteady hand, he placed the razor against the flesh just above my left ankle.

"No, Daddy, please. I'll be the only one in my class at school . . ."

He inched a wavy path up my leg. On the second pass, the razor skimmed the flesh along the shinbone like a skipped rock across the surface of a creek. Blood appeared and slowly fanned out, coursing down my leg. The sight of it made me seize up and hold my breath. Silent tears began to spill. Then I disengaged from my body and floated upward toward the sputtering fluorescent light above the sink. From the ceiling, I watched his hand glide in slow motion, row by row, exposing a bare calf.

Sometime before he finished the first leg, Mom shifted her weight and I looked up at her, back in my body again. *Look at me,*

Mom. Help me. Help ME. But I couldn't connect with her. Mom was reaching into her pants pocket for a cigarette and match.

On the next swipe, Dad's hand moved toward, up, and over my kneecap. I closed my eyes and bit down hard on my bottom lip. I prayed, *God, are you there? Please help me.* It was all I knew to do.

In one swift moment, I was divested of a growing sense of self, of independence, of control of my life, of trust. Just because he had the power, my father made me suffer at his ruthless hands and reduced me to shame, disgust for my body, and fear. I lost my childhood, my confidence, my faith in others. The following day during p.e. class in the gym, I was found out and my friends ridiculed my shaven legs.

June 2006

Contact with another researcher, this one in Jackson, resulted in finding newspaper accounts that were posted in the *Vicksburg Evening Post* and the Jackson *Clarion*. So it was really true. Another layer of denial melted away when I realized that three newspapers covered the story. Word had traveled all over the Delta that Dad was implicated. But as I read these accounts, looking for clues, I only found minor additions.

The Jackson paper ran the story under the headline "Negroes Killed but Officers Secretive." The district attorney from Vicksburg had not made his investigation yet so had no remark; Sheriff Crawford, who arrested Dad, was out of town and unreachable; the mayor of Anguilla spoke of the "three white brothers" as if he did not know them when in fact he was their uncle; the deputy at the sheriff's office said, "I don't know anything about it."

It was odd that all three papers made the statement that no racial issues were involved and that both black men were shot once each, in the front. Why would it be important to include those details if they were in fact true?

I made a call to my ex-husband at his law office and later faxed him Dad's letters from Africa and the newspaper accounts. He got right back to me with pertinent legal information—just as I knew he would. After all the years we had been married he cared about Dad even though he didn't respect him.

"This is fascinating stuff. His letter has so many currents, some more sympathetic than others. A youth at war suddenly handed such responsibility; a combat-bloodied idealist thrust into a role he did not see or want but knowing he had to be a 'man' and take care of the family; the unspeakable fear of having responsibility assigned to you by a demanding mother and expectant society while knowing she would not relinquish to you the real authority to do the job.

"The *Delta Democrat Times* has this as a sub-banner: 'Clean-up Was Editor's Aim.' In other words, the brothers were on a do-good mission. This sets up the defense. Also, in the same article, read the last paragraph. None of the participants were attached to the sheriff's office. Think about why the sheriff's office would release a statement saying that. In those days in those areas, members of the sheriffs' departments were involved in racial violence."

Yes, I thought, Dad was on a mission that night—ostensibly to shut down the juke joint and end the blacks' ready access to alcohol. He fully expected that he could, with his brothers by his side, demand that the patrons go home. He expected them to get up and leave just because he told them to. But black servicemen had served with other blacks from all over the country. Their sense of power became very different. When back on the home front, the rules changed again. And they'd changed for Dad too. He was no longer the homesick twenty-year-old who wrote letters home from Africa. In four years, dramatic shifts in his thinking had occurred, yet, that night, his arrogance and entitlement were enhanced by alcohol. The Pan Am station had a reputation for violence. It wasn't safe for Dad, Bill, and Tom to go there. They were foolishly living out their war mentality. On the night of December 12, 1946, spontaneous combustion was set off by testosterone, guns, old feuds, new ones, and alcohol. The end result was disaster.

☙❧

My ex-husband also explained to me the manner in which a grand jury operates. First, the proceedings are kept secret. Second, the jurists do not indict, they only determine if there is enough evidence against the defendant to take to trial. If they do make that determination, they return a "true bill" and if they don't, a "no true bill" is returned. He closed by saying, "A good district attorney can convince a grand jury to indict a ham sandwich."

I only knew that there had been no trial after the hearing. The bail money of five thousand dollars had been returned to Mamaw. Finding the paperwork from Sheriff Crawford, T. J. Lawrence, and Dr. Goodman was going to be important, but in the end, impossible. It was Dr. Goodman who pronounced Simon Toombs and David Jones dead and who attended to Uncle Tom's wounded shoulder.

Until now, I had focused my inquiry on the ways the event had affected my family. What about the men who were shot? I went online to search for army enlistment records and contacted the Mississippi State Department of Health, Vital Records, for certificates of death. The archives yielded much more information for a family name like Toombs. Not so for Jones. But the 1930 census did provide some details.

David Jones was born in Alabama. He moved to Mississippi and married Lizzie Carter in December 1929, taking her daughter by a previous marriage, Josephene, as his own. He was a tenant farmer in Anguilla and rented his home on the Sunflower River plantation. In subsequent research, I was unable to discover any further details of David's life because of the commonness of his name.

Simon Toombs was born January 15, 1911. He was a native of the Delta, worked as a tractor driver, and remained a bachelor until the final months of his life. In March of 1941, he enlisted in the U.S. Army and reported for duty at Camp Shelby. He was five feet ten and weighed 158 pounds when he entered the service. Simon returned to Anguilla in the summer of 1946 after serving for five years. He planned to marry a woman by the name of Sadie Gallion, but their marriage certificate was voided within a couple of months. He returned it to the magistrate at the Sharkey County Courthouse. Neither David nor Simon could write their own names. His death certificate indicates that the immediate cause of death was "a gun shot wound (penetrating) his chest" at 9:00 p.m. on the twelfth day of December.

Now I had a mental picture to go along with the names of the dead. Soon, I would get to know Simon much better through members of his extended family, still alive.

CHAPTER EIGHT

Undertow

July 2006

For as long as I can remember, my father drank. When we were young children in Knoxville, he often displayed a youthful vibrancy. The mood changes that occurred in him when he had consumed too much slipped by me without much notice. What did register was the way his habit affected my mother's mood. She was also a drinker who enjoyed her evening snort, but it was different. Her unhappiness was not limited to the time of day. Now, as I considered the family secret and how it had smoldered in a corner of their minds, I looked more intently at my parents' personality traits and began to consider the possibility that Dad enhanced his ability to forget the past by drinking himself away from it.

❦

In 1963, our family moved to Bristol, Virginia, just at the onset of my teenage years. Jay, Laura, and I were familiar and comfortable with our new hometown because our maternal grandparents, Mary and Joe Fleming, lived there and we visited them often. On an early visit, Daddy Joe, jovial and lighthearted, drove Jay and me to town to run an errand. He parked his black Cadillac in front of the Dominion Bank Building where he had an office, and then he coaxed us out into the middle of State Street, stopping the few oncoming cars with authority.

"Molly, Jay, come here. Look." He pointed down at evenly spaced brass markers embedded in the center of the road. "One side says, 'Bristol, Tennessee,' and the other side says, 'Bristol, Virginia.'"

"You mean," Jay said as he straddled the line, "I am standing in two states at the same time?"

I looked down and wondered how one town could have two names.

Bristol began as an outpost on the Norfolk and Western Railroad and flourished into a cultural mecca and commerce center for the southern Appalachians. Although urban renewal brought about the demise of many of the fine older buildings that were erected in the heyday of the town, the train depot, both post offices (vastly appealing in their architecture), two theatres, and a few other buildings were remaining vestiges of a grander time. They were in dire need of attention. The offices of both city governments were moved to boxy, modern brick quarters. Scattered throughout downtown were large empty lots that once lent their space to multistoried old hotels, the Harmeling Opera House, the YMCA organized in 1884, the home of Major A. D. Reynolds, who built his tobacco empire there. There were even a couple of recording studios that produced the first records of country music for musicians like Jimmie Rodgers, the Carter family, and Flatt and Scruggs.

Residential areas fanned out north and south of the state line with expansive tree-lined boulevards like Euclid Avenue in Virginia and Edgemont Avenue in Tennessee. Plenty of early twentieth-century bungalows, some large stately homes, and newer, less interesting houses were sprinkled into seasoned neighborhoods. One or two serious architects had designed unique yet mildly eclectic homes for wealthy residents.

Daddy Joe said, "Yes, and look, quick, down the street. See that sign? It was put up there just a year or so before I moved here from Georgia to marry your grandmother." Its arched steel frame was constructed in 1910. Attached white lights spelled out the city name with red arrows pointing down to either side of the street.

Virginia. Tennessee. In the dark of night, the yellow star in the middle flashed and it was possible to read the message: A Good Place to Live.

⚜

After Dad accepted a job as marketing director at Mary Grey Hosiery Mills, we arrived in town in the family's loaded-down Chevy Bel Air with my mother driving. My younger sister, Laura, was eight, and Jay was enrolled in boarding school in Orange, Virginia. Laura and I would begin that year as students in the public schools. Bristol was like Knoxville in that blacks resided in their own part of town and rarely crossed paths with whites except as domestic help.

Once settled in Bristol, I felt apprehensive, not only because I was leaving the familiar behind, but also because of a gnawing awareness of the widening crack in the foundation of my family. Despite my fears, a certain eagerness and anticipation accompanied me as we drove up to our new house that Dad chose to rent in a neighborhood north of town. He was there waiting for us. My guess is that he needed some insulation from my mother's parents, and so chose to settle on the Virginia side of town with a plan to relocate to a more permanent address later. I was a little surprised by the plainness of our new home. It had a typical 1950s design, brick halfway up the walls, then white siding. It rested on a low knoll facing Long Crescent Drive, approached by a driveway on the right side. A sidewalk linked the car park to the front porch. The roofline had a high pitch because there was a second, unfinished floor we would later use as an attic. With no dormer windows on the front, the house appeared to be just one level. The backyard was more appealing, with a flagstone patio enclosed by a three-foot-high brick wall, and steps leading up into a grassy area bordered by hemlocks. Very private. Later, we set out our butterfly chairs with dark blue canvas covers, our director's chairs, and a concrete birdbath, and eventually Mom put in a flower garden.

Beneath the main living area was the garage where Dad kept the tools he never used, trash cans, and occasionally the car. On the side of the house built into the bank was a large, unfinished room with a casement window that looked out onto the driveway and a door providing access to a stairway that led to the upstairs hallway. This area was given the name "game room," though it remained empty until the summer.

Once my family life resumed its normal pace I felt the old order resume, but there was a mean undertow sucking at us. I watched while Dad, who would have called himself a "social drinker" since he was off to the office bright and early every day and home from work at dusk for the five o'clock "tea" time, upped his consumption, and Mom became increasingly miserable in her life with him.

In our new house the kitchen was an extension of the dark, wood-paneled den. Today, the two areas together would be called a great room. There was a brick fireplace in the den and on either side of it were bookcases where we shelved all of Dad's Book-of-the-Month Club selections, his complete set of Rudyard Kipling works, the encyclopedia, and various other novels and history books. A couch and several upholstered chairs were set in place to create a comfortable area for my parents to sit after work when they were getting along. Or, if Mom was preparing dinner, Dad sat within her view and read.

The first thing he did after walking in the door in the evening was to shed his business suit. Then he joined Mom in the kitchen where he drew two highball glasses from the cupboard and enticed her, without much effort, to join him for a drink. There was a quantitative difference in how they drank. Dad carefully measured out two ounces of gin and poured it over the ice in Mom's glass. Then he filled it up with tonic. For himself, he would pour vodka into the two-ounce jigger while holding it over his glass so that he could continue to pour the vodka at the same time that he emptied the jigger. Then he would give his glass a splash of water. The jigger was just an accoutrement of drinking for him. While Mom sipped, he gulped. Some nights he had a hollow leg, could carry on a thoughtful conversation, and seemed himself. On those evenings, I could ask him a question and expect an answer. When he looked at me, he looked into my eyes. I actually liked it when he drank like that, because our connection was more normal and casual.

On other nights, he became different with the first drink. His talk became more boastful. He was full of bravado. He might say something like, "Those idiots at the newspaper don't have a goddam idea how to write." Or "I could straighten out this mess at the hospital in a one-hour meeting." Always, it was an institution that he was after. They were pretty much all poorly run and unfair to the general public, especially the federal government with all of its agencies. During these conversations, if that's what they were, Dad and I had no common ground. It was as if I wasn't in the room. My eyes opened wider with each change of topic. Even at fourteen, I could sense his ego becoming more and more inflated. I could hear the sarcasm and negativity in his speech. Before the end of the second drink, Dad's language would begin to slur. He had a penchant for using sophisticated vocabulary and for trying his hand at foreign words, never mind that he hadn't studied the language.

On one occasion, when Dad took us out to dinner at the Greek restaurant, he ordered a bottle of Chianti before the meal and a plate of antipasto. He had time before the food came to swill down three glasses of wine. Later, after we ate, when the waiter came to ask how we liked our food, Dad said, "C'est manifiqua!" The waiter left the table rolling his eyes, and I looked down into my lap.

Occasionally, if Dad had his first couple of drinks while changing out of his office clothes, he would come into the kitchen in his boxer shorts, tee shirt, and socks. He was five feet eleven and tended to be stocky. I knew to make myself scarce or at least to tiptoe around him when he began to knock about in the kitchen, banging the refrigerator shut so that the whole appliance rocked on its skinny supports. He'd slam a cabinet and sometimes something would break.

I pitied him at those times for two reasons. First, he looked oafish and stupid banging around like that. Second, he invoked my mother's wrath. Initially, she got quiet and drew back from him. Her face lost all signs of affect, her body stiffened. Then she came out of her corner striking like a cobra. The force of words between them became charged, heavy and hot. Mom kept a grocery list of Dad's wrongdoings. She used them against him when she was angry with him.

"Jay, you couldn't fix *anything* around here if you tried. I still can't believe you shortened the cord on the toaster so much that the plug wouldn't reach the socket anymore." Or, "Oh, here we go again, telling the same old story for the hundredth time." Or, "When are you going to mow the grass? The yard's an embarrassment. I'm tired of looking at it."

His customary retort: "Goddamnit, Betsy, what do you expect? You've castrated me. I try to teach Jay some responsibility . . . I ask him to mow. Then you tell him he doesn't have to do it. Mow the yard yourself."

While these arguments were escalating, I could feel myself shrink inside my own skin. I became smaller and quieter and meeker. I felt less sure, more fearful, ashamed, guilty, and helpless.

Sometimes Dad's glassy eyes spilled over into tears. He would become maudlin, weepy and remote. This behavior bred the same disdain in Mom that she had for his other drinking personae.

The tension between them was palpable. My fear made me feel somehow at fault. Like most teenagers, I had my share of hubris and it swelled just as Dad's did. I thought that if I just got it right, if I just did everything perfectly, Dad would be different and Mom would love him again. In a conversation with Mom years later, she told me that when she fell in love with Dad, she didn't want a marriage . . . she only wanted a wedding; that the relationship lost its glow in no time and my dark and robust father with a Mississippi drawl, fresh from serving in the army air corps, fell out of favor. She realized that my grandmother was not her idea of a mother-in-law. And she could never again go back to the thrill of living in New York City, single, with her girlfriends.

Mom probably tolerated Dad's drinking because both of her parents were drinkers and she liked it too, but for her, it created the perfect environment in which to level her complaints. She blamed Dad for everything that was wrong. Everything. And after listening to her criticism for a time, I, too, began to see his ineptitude while drinking as a sign that there was something lacking in his makeup, some moral weakness that contributed to his behavior.

⚭

Mom was fastidious about her appearance and kept herself neatly "together" at all times. She gave off an aura of sophistication, with her high forehead, arching cheekbones, and short patrician nose. She began each day with a bath and a fresh coat of pancake makeup, with eyeliner, mascara, and lipstick. Then she teased her streaked hair and combed it exactly the same way every day. She wore skirts and sweaters until the late '60s when women began to wear pants as part of their daily wardrobe. Dad towered over Mom a good seven or eight inches, but her energy level matched, if not surpassed, his. It was as if someone wound her up at the start of the day and she was launched about the house. She ticked off her chores with all the joy of a garbage collector. I imagined she was saying to herself, "It's Monday, strip the beds, run three loads of laundry, go to the grocery store, sweep the stoop, go by the church for altar guild duty, make phone calls for the history club, fix supper . . . and when Jay comes home from work, ask him how his day went, even though he won't bother to ask me about mine."

While Mom was using up her nervous energy during the day, Dad was at work at his new job. It seemed a good fit for a man who spent a number of years in the newspaper and advertising businesses. He designed ad campaigns for new lines of hosiery that came out each year. Frequently, he came home with thin, six-by-eight-inch boxes of hose for me and Mom. At first, I wore them with a garter belt which felt like a torture device. Later, Mary Grey produced panty hose and other leggings, like tights with geometric designs that Dad created. He went after his work in the same way he always had—with intensity. He didn't miss a day. And in that first spring in Bristol, he had plenty to talk about with Mom when he came home. But Dad was absent from his children whether or not he was at work. As I leaned into adolescence in this new town, I felt I needed an ally and Dad was not available. I needed him for strength and guidance. And I needed Mom for love and understanding. She was a good mother in the sense that she provided for my basic needs and comfort. Her eye for beauty, her stylish ways, and her sociability with peers were lost on me at that age. Due to my sensitive nature, I easily personalized the anger that seemed directed at me. I had a deep sense that nothing about me pleased her. In physical appearance, I favored my Dad—dark brown hair, brown eyes, and similar mouth. But it was my moodiness and self-absorption that most galled her.

❧

The first spring in our new house, two signs of hope emerged along with the bright yellow flowers on the forsythia bush. Our family joined the parish at Emmanuel Episcopal Church as soon as we settled in Bristol. When Ash Wednesday came that year, Dad went to church and made the decision to give up alcohol for Lent. For six weeks, he abstained from drinking, and he did it with aplomb. His spirits were good; he was available; I began to hope that he would find his respite so beneficial that he would give up drinking permanently. We attended church every Sunday during Lent. Dad didn't slip once that I knew about.

Right about that time, one of my mother's friends came by the house to ask for help with her spring showing of Doncaster ladies' wear. She had two or three clothing shows in her home every year. Some women in the town eschewed the two local dress shops and department stores to try on the expensive custom line of clothes.

Mom agreed to help out and, for three days, she stayed away. She helped ladies find their sizes and suggested outfits that would suit their coloring and shape. She was paid a commission for this. At the end of the show, Mom was asked if she would like to become a partner. She was thrilled and came home happy and proud of her work. She had helped her friend have one of her most successful seasons and she realized she had a knack for dressing other women.

When Lent culminated in Easter Sunday, Dad proved to himself, once again, that he didn't have a problem with alcohol; he could take it or leave it. Anyone who doubted him just damn well better take note that for six weeks he hadn't touched a drop. To celebrate his success, he mixed his usual vodka with a splash right at five o'clock and resumed his daily intake without a second thought.

Mom, visiting with my grandfather one Sunday afternoon, said, "Oh, Dad, I've just had a wonderful week helping my friend with her clothing business. She asked me if I wanted to take over for her. It would be so great for me, give me something to do, and a way to make a little spending money. I'm thinking about it."

"Over my dead body," my grandfather said. "You are a wife and mother of three children. It is inappropriate for you to go to work now. We are not in a position where you need to have a job. Tell her no, you are not available."

"But Dad, I need something to do. The kids are growing up. Jay's away at Woodberry. Molly's a teenager and Laura is no trouble now. I want to have something to do." I could sense Mom's bitter disappointment. She was bored and frustrated with her life. Any change would have helped.

Mom told me, later, that her parents were very generous with her. Her father gave her stocks and bonds over the years. She used the dividend checks to clothe my brother, sister, and me. When we lived in Knoxville, she sold all of her assets to help Dad invest in a housing development and start up an advertising agency, McCabe and Fields. But Daddy Joe replenished her investments. As with most of my Dad's "projects," the development didn't take hold. Only three houses were built during the time we lived there.

But Dad gave Mom money out of his paycheck for groceries. He would tell her that he paid the phone bill, but often she would get a call that the phones would be cut off the following day. She bailed him out again and again. After the move to Bristol, Dad depended on his father-in-law to keep the family afloat. His drinking made him less and less responsible with money.

Because of Daddy Joe's generosity and his dominance, Mom felt beholden to follow his lead. When he said she could not have a job, my mother was crushed. She never forgave him for that. Though she loved her parents and had always felt especially close to her father, his insistence that she not work put a strain on their relationship.

☙

The more time I spent getting to know my new neighbors, the more I realized that Bristol was a petri dish growing an alcohol culture. No one ever used the word "alcoholic" to identify the family drinkers. It seemed as if all of the grown-ups were doing it. What else could they do in a town of forty thousand with no way to socialize outside of a cocktail party? Though my parents' drinking life wasn't viewed as excessive by our neighbors and friends, I remained hypervigilant.

And I watched all of the neighbors as well. Dad's boss, Bill Kramer, lived next door. He and his wife, Katie, had a snootful every evening. They were Mississippians and had three daughters and one son, Josh, older than I. Our neighbors on the other side were the Cunninghams. They had a daughter, Lynn. She was my age, shorter than I, with pretty shoulder-length blonde hair and an eye that strayed into the periphery of her field of vision. This defect was a source of embarrassment to her and it required several surgeries that cost her clear vision out of that eye. She was open to friendship and I soon learned that because she went to St. Anne's Catholic School, she was smart. She ate fish every Friday and wore a mantilla to mass. Her parents didn't agree on things any more than mine did, but they had open confrontations that somehow got resolved, unlike my parents' arguments that always ended in bitter silence. Her dad, Jerry, a local CPA (the Catholic parent), insisted that his children go to church. Her mother, Mary Viola, was a short, irreverent, and feisty woman with a gimp leg. She didn't give a damn whether Lynn went to confession or not. She had three other children to worry about, two older, one younger. She also had a serious passion for bridge and her glass of wine. Jerry was a routine drinker, too. Because of that it was okay, in the beginning, for Lynn to come to my house. It didn't matter to her that my parents were drinking, that my dad could be boisterous and loud. My mother became charming and funny when outsiders were around. Lynn loved her. Once Mom was commenting on a neighbor who was a penny-pincher. She told Lynn, "He's so tight, two nickels would squeak in his pocket."

The Goodpastures, who lived across Long Crescent from Lynn's family, were social drinkers, too. They had a son, Frank, who was a year older than I and a daughter, McLean, who was a year younger. "Lean" was pretty, musically talented, and loved horses. Her family had an aristocratic Virginia bearing, while the Cunninghams were a noisy Kentucky presence on the street.

Lean and I walked the four blocks home from the junior high each afternoon. She told stories about the other kids in the neighborhood and I began to get my bearings and learn about sex. Neither one of my parents had ever discussed matters of intimacy. One of the first realizations I had, when I started school that winter at Virginia Junior High, was that my peers were far more mature than I, in more ways than one. Boys and girls were already "going together" and all of the cute ones were taken. I couldn't help developing a crush on Josh because he lived next door and was very tall and handsome with dark brown hair that fell over his left eye. He had broad shoulders and a swagger. He brought his right shoulder forward when he walked. Josh was already in high school and playing football that year. One day, when Lean and I were walking home from school, I confided in her that I "liked" Josh. She started to giggle.

"What's so funny?" I asked.

"Have you ever been in the Kramers' house?"

"Just the kitchen."

"Well, his room is upstairs on the front of the house. If you go outside at night, in the dark, and look up at his room, you might see him up there. He masturbates in front of the window. Believe me, I've seen him!"

"What do you mean, masturbates?"

"That's a word Frank taught me. Ask your brother when he comes home from school. He'll tell you."

It wasn't that hard to figure out what she was talking about.

ॐ

As the spring began to unfold and the days warmed, the neighborhood hummed with teenagers after supper every night. Kids came out of shadowy corners to converge on someone's expansive lawn until we had enough people to play hide-and-seek or freeze tag. Frank and Lean were there, and Lynn, Josh, and sometimes the Slacks, Miles, and Adams kids. I don't remember how we arrived at the rules but we confined our games to five or six yards. There were innumerable hiding places. Most of the older, two-story brick houses had garage apartments or sheds. There were driveways lined with giant boxwoods, terraced backyards, large hemlock or privet hedges. When I first started seeking out places to hide, I felt overwhelmed by the maze of our neighborhood. But I soon learned to negotiate it and I learned who was really fast on his feet and who might try to cop a feel behind Mrs. Parks's house. She was too old and deaf to even know we were there. But it was really important not to raise the hackles of her next-door neighbor, Downman Mitchell. He and his beautiful, white-haired wife, Eileen, were also leaning into old age pretty hard. Mrs. Mitchell had rheumatoid arthritis and was turning into an invalid. Mr. Mitchell, the first grown-up I knew who had attended an Ivy League school, Princeton, never slept and was liable to come out shouting. He inflicted serious verbal abuse when he was drinking. After dark, we drifted to our respective homes and settled down for homework or television.

The next morning we were back in school. When I entered the junior high at midyear, I had no friends. Cliques had already formed. Someone told me about a shoplifting ring made up of girls from upper-middle-class families. They walked the eight or so blocks to town after school and made their rounds at the H. P. King Department Store, Belk, and Woolworth's, nonchalantly picking up and pocketing items like lipstick, nail polish, bubble gum, and costume jewelry. When I asked who these girls were, I learned they were cheerleaders, class officers, members of the country club. I found this incomprehensible. My father caught me in a lie once, and we sat down for a "talk." I would rather have my mother take a belt to me than have to face my father and "'fess up." Still, I was in awe of these girls who were bold enough to rip off local businesses. How gutsy. How brazen.

At the same time, I heard tales about the neighborhood boys. Our house had been unoccupied for a number of months during the previous summer. Frank Goodpasture and his cousins had stood atop our house on Long Crescent Drive and nailed cars with eggs. The mayor of Bristol drove by one evening and caught a half dozen on his windshield and other parts of his car. This gave the boys serious bragging rights and they were undeterred by whatever consequences awaited them.

I also observed how much pride my Bristol peers took in wearing Weejuns with no socks, madras shorts, and shirts with Peter Pan collars for girls, or button down for boys. One day after I entered a stall in the girls' bathroom and latched the door, I heard the voices of several of the popular girls. One said, "Have you seen the new girl?" "Yeah, she's from Knoxville." "Can you believe she still wears those white ankle socks?" "What a freak!" That was followed by laughter.

When the bell rang at the end of school that day, I mustered my books and walked mostly uphill toward home. Lean walked with me along Lawrence Avenue with its canopy of branches and leafy limbs. At home, I retreated into the living room which could be made private by shutting the swinging doors that led into the den and kitchen. There I could take refuge in my first love, music. My Fleming grandparents had given me a Knabe baby grand piano for a Christmas gift when I was ten. The size and weight of this gift filled me with excitement and deep gratitude. At last someone had heard my pleas to take music lessons. It also made me feel obligated to "perform," to come out of hiding. I dutifully practiced scales and played Bach inventions every day. Mom asked Mrs. Goodpasture who was teaching Lean's piano lessons. She was referred to Ralph Ostoff, who taught in the music department at Virginia Intermont College, three blocks from our house. Mr. O was one of a handful of openly gay men living in Bristol at the time. Tall and fiftyish, he was at first kind and encouraging to his new, shy student. His flair for the dramatic was interesting to me. He sang along with me as I played and sometimes he conducted, waving a pencil in the air in time to the melody. I learned how to subtly engage my whole body in the making of music and how to bring heart to it. On lesson days, I walked to his house where he lived with his mother on Harmeling Street. The rooms were full of Victorian furniture in deep crimson tones of velveteen fabric. Light filtered in through windows covered with sheers. Because of him, I developed a love of the piano and the cadence and lilting qualities of my music. For some reason, my mother never felt inclined to interfere with my practice time. It was my own.

Laura was the only one who gave me a hard time about the cacophony that emerged from the living room when I played. After the move to Bristol, our rivalry came into full flower. Age barred her from the teenage gang in the neighborhood. She had to seek out friends down the street, in a younger set. At eight, she was blonde, blue-eyed, outspoken, and athletic. Mom could find her on any given afternoon skateboarding down the sidewalk with the boys her age. She was fearless. One day a week, Laura and her friends met at the Arnolds' house in the garage apartment for the Horse Lover's Club. I don't know what they did there, but Lean was usually in charge and the members wore their jodhpurs to meetings.

Neither Lynn nor I was into horses, so we holed up in her room and talked about what was going on at school, who was dating whom, which couples had "gone all the way." We denied Laura access to our discussions. This was my first experience of privilege by virtue of age. Whenever Mary V. let Laura come into the house, she tapped on the door of Lynn's room and said, "Molly, Lynn, let Laura in. She has a joke for you."

"Go away, Laura," we shouted in unison. If she persisted and we let her in, she spun a yarn until we grew bored with listening. Then she broke out in a paroxysm of laughter that we found unworthy of response. After that, we made her leave. Our brutal behavior brought on tears, and we knew she was sure to let Mom and Dad know about it.

One day I noticed Laura sneaking food out of the kitchen and disappearing outside. At first I thought she was meeting her friends for a snack too close to suppertime. Out of curiosity, I followed her out the back door and caught her hiding in the hemlocks that grew between our house and the Kramers'. Josh was wearing his dirty football jersey, carrying his helmet as he lumbered up his driveway. Laura stepped out of the hedges and extended a plate of stolen cookies to him. She had a lot of nerve going after my crush. I made note of the ease with which she could sneak past Mom. And I was jealous.

☙

As soon as I finished practicing the piano in the afternoons, I was open game for Mom's list of chores. By this time, we had a housekeeper, Anna Mae Cook, who lived near the projects in a ramshackle house where she raised eight children. Since I was rarely in the presence of African Americans outside of my home, this reinforced my elitist mentality. Mom and I had to prepare for Anna Mae at the end of the day. First, we had to pick up the house and neaten before she arrived so that her job would be easy. There were certain chores like washing windows and polishing silver that you just didn't ask "the help" to do. I hated it when the brass became tarnished, the silver dull. It meant standing beside Mom in the kitchen with no conversation except the occasional "you missed a spot." A great conflict grew up within me. A much younger version of myself prodded me to get it done quickly, forget about being perfect. The inner critic spoke up just in time and said, "Slow down, cover all of the surface—rub hard, make it shine. She'll be happy. You won't have to do it over and you can go outside sooner." Despite the battle, a still louder voice was chanting in the silence. "I hate this. I hate silver. I hate standing beside you. I hate being the one you pick on, I hate you."

In mid-May, my brother came home from Woodberry Forest School with a carload of dirty clothes. Right away, I noticed how he had changed. Taller, more muscular, with a shadow of facial hair that matched his straight and dark brown mop, he was clean cut and a bit quiet. He quickly moved into his room at the end of the hall and took up his place in the family as the golden child. In short order he was driving out to the golf course to play eighteen or even thirty-six holes during the day. I was glad to have him back if for no other reason than to break the monotony at home. My parents insisted that he get a job that summer, so he and Josh worked on Judge Widener's cabin on Holston Lake. They shoveled mud out of the basement during the day with intermittent dips in the cool lake water. Then, at night, they joined the rest of us playing in the dark out in the neighborhood.

One evening, not long after Jay returned home, I sat at the dinner table listening.

"Mom and Dad, I like it here, in Bristol. I don't want to go back to Woodberry in the fall. I want to stay here and go to the high school."

I wondered what it was like at Woodberry Forest for Jay to give up the experience of going there.

Several minutes of silence were followed by Dad's response. "Jay, you stand a much better chance of getting into a good college if you stay in boarding school. Your grandmother shipped me off to Riverside Academy in Georgia when I was fourteen and I went from there to Davidson College."

"But Dad, Josh and Frank are trying to get me to play football. I can make good grades here. I'm sure I can."

"Jay," Mom chimed in, "Mam and Joe are paying for you to go to Woodberry. I think they'd be disappointed if you didn't go back. Stop raring back in your chair."

For several weeks, there was no resolution to this show-down. Jay's tactic was to press hard against Mom, knowing she would cave in. When she did, my parents entered one of their distant periods of little communication and lots of tension. I was dismayed when things didn't improve, even though Jay was distracting my parents from me and Laura, and I relished watching someone else in the hot seat.

During that year I brought home a report card that had more Bs than As. Dad and I had a little talk about it. "It's not a bad report, Molly. You are a good, hard worker, but you'll never be as smart as your brother." I felt the sting of his remark. I tried to mitigate his criticism by remembering that he brought home a special gift for me from one of his New York business trips. It was a microscope in a wooden box. I had no interest in science until then. *Dad must think I'm smart enough to use this microscope. Maybe he doesn't think I'm a lost cause.*

৵৹

Some nights after supper, Jay left with friends to go to Shorty's Pool Hall. Laura ran out the back door to play at the Wamplers' house. It was my job to help with the supper dishes. I collected them from the table, scraped and stacked them on Mom's side of the sink. I found a dry tea towel and took hold of each clean plate as she passed it under the faucet. No matter how long it took her to wash, I stood there waiting, usually looking out the kitchen window to the patio and the birdbath just opposite the window, observing the lengthening shadows as dusk fell. Over the spring and summer months I studied the birds that flew into and out of the yard—especially the chickadees and titmice. I knew the house wrens and towhees and jays because my grandmother sat with me in front of her bay window where we could see her birdfeeders. She named each bird that flew in for dinner.

For several weeks a baby bird swooped from branch to branch in a tree next to the patio. It didn't take long before it was visiting the rim of the birdbath. Soon, it learned how to hop into the shallow basin and flutter itself wet.

"Look, Mom, that's the same little wren that's been coming to the birdbath every evening." I knew it by its head movements and its standard perch on the rim.

"You don't know that's the same bird, Molly. Don't be ridiculous."

We were not on unfamiliar ground but that particular exchange has stayed in my mind. Before that, I accepted her perspective without question, for fear of making her angry. I had no regard for my own ability to perceive the truth. For the first time, I didn't get hung up on the word *ridiculous* and how I would have to try to eradicate that quality from my person. A deep sadness came over me and I questioned, *Why can't Mom see into the heart of a thing?*

❧

In June, my best buddy from Knoxville called from a pay phone somewhere in Bristol. "Molly, this is Pam. My parents and I are driving through on our way home from Washington, D.C ."

"Pam! I haven't made many friends here yet. I miss you."

"My parents said we could stop by to see you. Just for a few minutes."

I turned to Mom, put my hand over the receiver and asked if it would be okay.

"No, not today. We have too much to do."

I turned back to the phone, "Pam, I'm sorry but Mom says it won't be convenient this time. I hope I can come down to Knoxville soon to see you. We had so much fun in Girl Scouts. I really miss everybody. Do you still have my address? I'll write to you."

When I hung up the phone, I slowly turned in my mother's direction. Loneliness, frustration, and anger coalesced in my body. I remember shouting at her, the words leaping from my mouth like flames licking the inside walls of a house on fire. In that instant, I was no longer fourteen; I was speaking and acting like a five-year-old child who thought her words had immense power.

Mom stopped, looked at me, lowered her chin, and seemed to grow an inch or two taller. "Don't you ever, ever talk to me like that again, young lady." And she stalked out of the room. Dad did his usual thing. He lifted the newspaper in front of his face so as to become invisible. He was no help at all.

Looking back on that event, I see that it was not the language or our argument that had emotional weight for me. It was the fact that Mom walked out of the kitchen and into her bedroom. She shut the door and went to bed. We didn't see her again until the next morning when she would not look at me. Did my anger make her physically ill? That was the first time I was aware of my own rage. It scared me. Never again would there be a confrontation like that one. I had to find more subversive ways to make her suffer, to confound her, to survive living with her like two magnets with opposite poles, stored in the same box.

As an adult woman, a mother, and a wife, I grew to understand the exhaustion born out of the unhappiness that my mother must have felt. It would have taken all of her strength and energy to resist my father's domination and his real or imagined potential for harm.

CHAPTER NINE

Revelations

July 16, 2006

I set the trip odometer at zero, locked my doors, and positioned the map of Mississippi on the passenger seat. I decided to take the southern route through Atlanta, but I only made it into South Carolina before stopping at a busy new gas station where I bought a pack of cigarettes, the first in a number of years. I would deal with the guilt later; smoking would ease the tension and make the miles go by faster.

I was relieved that Jay was not along on this trip. He was swept up in caring for his new girlfriend who had breast cancer. They were preparing to go to Rochester to the Mayo Clinic. Leaving South Carolina, I eased the first CD of Anne Tyler's new book-on-tape into the player and buzzed on down the road, driving all day until I reached Yazoo City.

I saw enough of the town to surmise that, like Anguilla, it was predominantly black. A little chill rose up my spine when I thought about being alone in a hotel room. Once inside, I wedged a chair-back under the doorknob and settled. I was only just beginning to reckon with my own internalized racial fear and the effects of white privilege. Avoiding blacks was something I had done without thinking. I'd chosen to move from my postseparation apartment into a gated community where I lived for almost a year before it began to feel stifling. I didn't think about what it would be like to be rejected because of my skin color. All my life, doors had opened for me that would have remained closed for blacks and other ethnic groups. But, on this day, I was one of the minority races in the Mississippi Delta and I felt vulnerable.

The fears I had were of multiple origin. They were strong enough to subvert rational thought. Most women fear being alone in a hotel in the middle of nowhere. But racial fear went way back and was not gender based. I remembered how my grandmother managed her home with the authority and control of General George S. Patton. While she was in her kitchen, she didn't ask Mat or Jo to "please [or kindly] put the roast in the oven." But it was the tone of her voice rather than the words that brought about immediate compliance. They knew better than to trifle with Miss Beck, but I noticed and registered the seething anger that sometimes flickered in their eyes. Any sensitive child would have picked up on it. As an adult, I knew that Jo drank her anger down and Aunt Mat prayed it away.

ᘓᕀᘒ

The next morning the heat was oppressive, eighty-eight degrees at ten o'clock. I drove by Yazoo City's beautiful, gingerbread-encrusted Victorian homes—mostly white siding with turrets, and lazy rockers on front porches. Then I headed west, crossed the Amtrak rails. A huge chip mill off to the left caught my eye. When they finish deforesting this area, how many of these elegant trees will still be standing?

During the thirty miles it took to drive from Yazoo to Anguilla, I could study my map while driving. The road was flat and stretched out for miles behind and in front of the car. The crops, extending into the distance, were delineated by long strips of dark green hardwoods. Occasionally, a car or a truck passed me on the two-lane road, but mostly I saw straight vertical lines of corn, soybeans, and cotton baking in the direct light of the sun. I passed an odd sharecropper house, the occasional oasis of massive farming equipment, combines, harvesters, the like. I drove by mileage markers for such colorfully named towns as Midnight,

Belzoni, Nitta Yuma. My mind was absorbed in the view of the land made lush and verdant under the relentless shine of the sun, at ease in a cloudless sky.

The closer I came to my destination, the more timorous I felt. I remembered that Pat Thrasher and Mayor Richardson, both white, warned me that ninety-three-year-old King Evans was "racist." I didn't know if, when I visited him, he would see an opportunity to lash out at me about the horrible thing my father was said to have done. My heart pounded and anxiety buzzed in my ears when I parked on Second Street in front of his aging white bungalow. I was about to enter, for the first time in my life, the home of a black family. His daughter, Carolyn, met me.

After she swung open the screen door, she said, "Welcome. Won't you come in?" She was a beautiful woman who had an aura of gentility and high-mindedness. She introduced me to her father, her mother, and her brother, King, Jr. Right away, I noticed the video camera aimed at the corner of the room where I would sit and where King sat in his recliner. I was ushered to the last cushion on the sofa. I carried a small recorder in my hand. He had one beside him, too. He was a handsome black man, thin, dressed in a blue striped shirt with pants held up by suspenders. He had graying hair and wore a black patch over his right eye. We plunged into conversation as if we had known each other for years. Despite his stuttering, I could make out most of what he said.

"Would you like to talk to me about what my father did?" I asked.

"Your daddy was all right, but, see, Mr. Bill was the first one to irrigate in this area. When I went down there and saw that stream of water I thought it had rained. Mr. Bill Fields was pumping water out of the creek to irrigate the cotton. He told me about his farming."

"King . . . answer her question," Mrs. Evans urged with her soft voice and gentle way.

"Well, well . . . ," he stuttered and then said, "Your daddy, H. J., well, see, I didn't know him very well. I believe Mr. H. J. was a little darker or a little rougher lookin'. I wasn't around him at all."

"My dad went away to school and then he went into the army air corps," I said. "When he came back here with my mother, they lived in the house next to Miss Rebekah's. My mom had my brother there, and he was just a baby when the shooting happened. Mr. Evans, you told me on the phone that you were coming back into town the night that Simon and David were killed." We talked about how Dad, Tom, and Bill left the scene but drove back by the Pan Am station later. King saw them slow and gape at the sight of Simon's body lying still on the ground. I thought, maybe they needed to be certain of what they had done.

King said, "I saw Simon fall. And I got to him. When I went to him he was taking his last breath. He didn't say a word.

"They were in the station. And the Fields boys came in and told them to go home. And they didn't want to go home. They had been hanging out there all the time and David usually kept a .45 automatic and so he didn't get his gun in time—I don't know. He attempted to get it and that's when they hit him I think—hit him on the head. But he was known to carry that automatic."

Then, King, Jr., leaned forward and emphatically said, "What I've heard over the years is that Mr. Bill Fields is the one that did the shootin'. Mr. Bill pulled the trigger." He looked into my eyes to register his point with me.

"*What?* Bill? Not my dad?" But when I glanced back at his father to see how this information sat with him, he rustled in his seat and said, "Bill looked like he was just there because they told him, Come on, Bill, let's go."

Another discrepancy. This was an enormous change. I felt at sea.

King, Jr., said, "I always thought that one shootin' involved self-defense but the other was just plain out murder because I never heard anything about Simon even having a gun and never known to carry a gun. So now with two dead men, you should have at least two guns. But they only found one gun. David Jones was known to have a gun and the only reason he got killed was because he didn't get his gun up fast enough to shoot first."

Changing the subject, King, Sr., said, "The proprietor disappeared before the trial. Pearson Blakely—he disappeared before the trial and they had a time finding him."

Neither King, Jr., Mrs. Evans, nor Carolyn said anything to contradict him, and we all waited for somebody else to speak. I scratched the itch on my left cheek, as I often do when nervous. I asked about the aftermath, the descendents, funerals, and burial plots. King told me that after the bodies were taken away, people just shut themselves up in their homes fearing that even the slightest move would look like retaliation. Neither Sheriff Crawford nor the white landowners would tolerate that. More black people would have died. Further, there was no discussion of the incident in the African American community. People were too shocked and too afraid. King continued on with faltering memory, and then he drifted off into details about the town and the area, and the attrition of the black population due to large, corporate farming.

I asked, "Do you think they just didn't want black people to have access to alcohol? It seems like a power thing to me."

Carolyn, whose kind, round face and soft eyes were animated when she spoke, said, "You have to remember that it was a controlled environment. What caused the brothers to decide to close an establishment that night, it might be something deeper than that."

King, Jr., asked, "Have you talked to Miss Rogers, Miss B. B.?"

"No, but I've heard her name mentioned before."

He continued, "She knows everybody around here and a lot of what went on."

We talked for two hours. Occasionally, I brought the conversation back to what happened. But they were interested in me, my children, my life. I gave King and Mrs. Evans a basket from the North Carolina farmers' market full of Mason jars with honey, pickled relish, and the like. I felt awash in gratitude. The warnings of two whites that Mr. Evans was racist were far from the truth. He was a remarkable man, both in his memory and in his fairness to all. His family had welcomed me into their home. They put me at ease and shared all the information they had. If only my family could understand why this incident was important to me. If only they could be as forthcoming as the Evans family.

After I left their house, I went to the Sharkey County Courthouse to see my friend Pat Thrasher. She was eager to know what I learned from King Evans. When I entered her office, she motioned to me with a crooked finger. I followed her into the corner of her office, past the piled-up desk, the copy machines, the coffee station, the filing cabinets.

She spoke in a hushed voice, leaning toward me. "I spoke with Charles Weissinger, the county attorney. He's the local historian and grew up in a family much like yours. He said that the story that came down to him was that the Fields men went to the gas station that night *looking* for Simon Toombs. He was your dad's half-brother."

CHAPTER TEN

Yet Another Version

Oh, my God. For the second time that day, my body registered new information with a shudder, my stomach tightening into a hard knot. My grandfather, whom I never knew, seemed to have been adored by his wife and children, though they rarely spoke of him. Had he cheated on my grandmother? Had he taken a black woman as his lover?

Pat continued, "It seems that your grandfather deeded land on the north side of Ashland Plantation to Simon. Your dad and his brothers went to the Pan Am station to kill him. It had nothing to do with alcohol." Before I could fully register what she said, she went on, "Now. Emma Harris called me while you were out. She found out about your being here, and she wants you to come to see her. Her mother and her aunt are Simon's nieces. Let me get her on the phone for you."

❧

On the way to Emma Harris's house, I bought a sandwich and a cup of coffee at a gas station. I took two Tylenol to slow down the express train headache coming on and an antacid tablet for the bile collecting in my stomach. I took out my notebook and wrote down Charles Weissinger's twist on the story. I had to clear my head. I had to find a way to be present mentally. More people. More stories. How much more outrageous could this tale become? I fought strong urges to shut down or throw up.

❦

I drove the five miles from Rolling Fork to Anguilla, smoking and hoping they wouldn't be able to detect the stench on my breath or clothing, hoping my tired bloodshot eyes wouldn't make me out to be as unhinged as I felt. I thought about how I didn't have time to be afraid. Women. They would be less threatening. But I braced myself when I pulled into the gravel driveway to the right of the small, pale blue house with bright blue trim. I hoped that no new information would surface.

Emma met me at the door. Though she was stockier than I, her lustrous, flawless skin disguised the fact that we were almost the same age. She introduced me to her mother, Rose Cooper, and to her aunt, Inez Files. We settled ourselves on the sofas in the living room where photos of Emma's grown son lined the mantle. It seems that there were lacy, crocheted doilies lying against the headrests of stuffed chairs, and a braided rug filled the space on the open floor.

Emma, the former and only black, only female mayor of Anguilla, spoke proudly of her accomplishments in bettering the education of black boys and girls. They asked about my family, my "chillen," a term my own grandmother lovingly used.

I looked from Emma to Rose, her mother, another large, dark-skinned, pretty woman. Inez, her sister, was taller, lean, with milk-chocolate skin and more angular features. She had the presence of an educator. Teaching high school English in Greenville for most of her life gave her an air of authority.

I recounted the story as I'd heard it.

Inez was first to speak. "From what I gather and I actually don't know—the Fields boys decided that they were going to close the town that night and my uncle and David Jones had just come back from the military and they were all sitting around the table drinking. And the Fields boys came in and said they were going to close the town. It always struck me as strange as to what authority did the Fields boys have to close the town. So they told my uncle and David Jones to leave and they said, 'We are going to leave as soon as we finish our drinks.' But they said, 'No, you are going to leave now,' and they told them to run and having just come back from fighting in the war—I guess to them it was different from what they had been doing and what they had been encountering and to come back home and not receive any kind of respect, you know. My husband talked about it but he said he actually saw it.

"Now, the only other thing I heard as a teenager was that my uncle Simon had this green field jacket, you know, the jackets that the soldiers wear, and my dad brought that jacket home and I can envision right now in my mind seeing those bullet holes in that jacket and the blood."

I interrupted her. "There was more than one hole?"

"Seems to have been three or four because they were sort of staggered. And not knowing this story would come back, we could have very easily kept the jacket but even as a ten-year-old it was a very traumatic experience. And you know all of the town's people were wondering what was going to be done about it and of course back then—you know what I'm talking about—when a black kills a black they get whatever—and even—I don't know whether—this is kind of off the subject but the lady who used to live over there—this black man and her husband had had an altercation and the black man killed him and this black man was dragged through Anguilla. He was already dead, I understand, when they did that but they literally dragged him through Anguilla. I said that to say. . . ."

"There was no justice," I finished.

Inez went on, "You read about the civil rights workers and different things like that. It was just an everyday thing—a common thing. You can empathize, being a human being, but there is no way that you can really understand it."

"That's right. I can't walk in your shoes." I glanced across the room to Rose. She was sniffling and wiping quiet tears from the corners of her eyes. I felt my heart sag deeper into my chest. And I was grateful when Emma offered to bring me a glass of cold water.

Inez moved forward on the couch and looked me straight in the eye. "And I want to tell you even after sixty years, I appreciate you having the integrity to want to know what happened. No more than for your own satisfaction."

I was thrown off guard by her remark and looked away. "I know about the injustice. I learned from my grandmother that even though she loved and cared for the people that worked for her, she had racism in her heart until the day she died. I can't imagine what you have been through living in a society like this."

"Oh, it's bad even now." Inez pointed to Rose. "That's my sister and complexion-wise I'm fairer than she is. We can go into a store together even in this day and time and if it's a white salesperson, they will wait on me before they do her."

Emma couldn't contain herself a moment longer. "I was told that Simon and David were shot down in cold blood because they wouldn't run."

"From the bullet holes," Inez went on, "apparently my uncle had to be shot in the back because the bullet holes in the front of the jacket would have had to have been larger."

And finally Rose spoke. "Uncle Simon was my favorite uncle. My daddy hung his jacket on the front porch so anybody passin' by could see it and Mamma said, 'Willie, you need to move that jacket. It's just disturbin' me.' And everybody would come by and my daddy would show them the jacket 'cause there were four witnesses up there that said that they all were sitting down drinking and having fun and they came in and was going to make them go home and by them being in service they said wait a minute, we ain't done nothing, why make us go home and they told him to shut up and then everybody got emotional of course cause they wouldn't run—would none of the rest of 'em run—that was what Willie was saying—he saw them. They were all going to stay and they just start shootin' but I ain't never heard nobody say that David pulled no gun. He didn't have no gun."

Inez continued, "What my husband used to say, he was sitting across the street from the Pan Am station and he saw it all because the way he would tell it, that the one they said did the shooting didn't."

I told the three women about what King, Jr., said, that Uncle Bill was the one that pulled the trigger.

"That is what my husband always said. Well, now, Bill was the youngest, wasn't he? And I mean, rationally I could see one of the older ones taking the rap for him. As I said, my husband is no longer with us but he always said that Bill was the one that pulled the trigger."

Now Rose entered. "When they sent for Daddy, he came back and said Bill Fields done shot Simon and my mother was scream-ing. We all was livin' on the plantation back then and my grand-mother was the cook for the white doctor—she lived over there by those trees. And we went over to see her and she of course was taking it hard and we all cried together." For Rose and Inez, only fond memories of Simon were on their minds. His nieces were only ten and twelve years old when he died. He was kindhearted to them. He was nice looking. He spent time talking to children so they looked up to him. After the military, he came home, a survivor, a hero.

The tragedy was becoming all too real at this moment. I felt such sadness for this family. I felt confused. Why would Dad take the blame and risk going to prison when he had a new wife and baby boy? Why did he keep the truth from my mother? Did he have some deeper guilt that was assuaged by sacrificing himself for his brother's sake? More than likely, he just trusted that the judicial system would not weigh in against him.

Inez told me that black families kept secrets too, but for dif-ferent reasons. "In a sense they were afraid. If they talked about it, they talked about it hush-hush among themselves because there could have been repercussions, because I know there were very few people that my husband told that he actually witnessed it. But he did say that somebody restrained him from coming home because he had a .45 in his mom's house to retaliate." She spoke again of the tragedy of Simon's and David's coming home from the service *just* to "get killed." Then she asked, "But does anybody know who the other witnesses were?"

Rose answered, "Yeah, but they dead. And you ain't goin to find no records nowhere."

We talked about the fact that the war was the beginning of many changes that came to the Delta. Inez spoke of her husband's experience. "He took most of his tour of duty overseas and he said all the way home all of the GI's were getting together laughing and talking and he said that the atmosphere changed as soon as they got to Camp Shelby."

Our conversation meandered from World War II to the Iraq War, from teaching to eliminating racism. Finally I realized that we were all getting tired, but I had one more weighty issue to raise, and it would elicit a strong reaction.

"I was told something that I've gotta put on the table. Charles Weissinger's version of what happened that night in '46 was that Simon was my father's half-brother." As I spoke these words, a chill ran up my spine. These women might be considered family.

Inez replied, "I never heard that before but it could very well have been true. My grandmother was a midwife and I'm not sure. I never heard anybody say that my grandmother assisted white women, but I know that there was another one who did. During that time, if a white man saw a black woman that he desired, he just took her. Even though I never heard of it and though all of my father's sisters and brothers are deceased, we don't have anybody to ask and of course I never heard that. Simon may have known about this but didn't tell anybody."

"Charles said that my grandfather deeded land at Ashland Plantation to Simon and that's why they shot him. I can't find any records." Questions surfaced about how the land passed down through my family, about my grandfather's will, and about Simon's portion. I would have to think about the significance of land and why it meant so much to Dad and his brothers. Clearly, for their forebears, land was hard won and a far more valuable asset than anything else. They'd prided themselves on the numbers of acres they were able to put together. The more land, the more status, power, and wealth. That some of it had been given away to an unknown heir, much less to a black one, would have been an incendiary inconvenience.

Emma seemed caught up in the possibility that there might still be a way for them to benefit. She said that if Charles Weissinger told this story then he might have proof. "The Weissinger family and the Fields family is of the same magnitude."

Inez tamped down the fervor that was rising in the room. "But see, Emma, during that time, I'm not saying he did, I'm not saying he didn't, but it may not have been put in writing." She went on, "But can't you imagine how traumatic this must have been to the Fields boys to realize that they had killed . . . no, I'm not sure—I never heard anybody say that when they decided to close the town that they actually knew the people were in the building—whoever they were. If this [story] is true, I would think from the fair skin and the occupation my grandmother had as a midwife and her working for two bachelors . . ." She was referring to Simon's fair skin color when she disappeared into her own thoughts.

❦

Before I left Emma's home, Inez encouraged me to follow my heart and get at the truth. "At the end of the day, if you pursue this, you are doing it because of the peace you need."

A fitful night produced wild dreams, sweaty sheets, and resolve. I dressed and packed and drove directly to the courthouse in Rolling Fork. The tomblike record room was quiet and I was alone. If my grandfather promised land to Simon there would be a deed. For the next two hours, I combed the heavy red leather deed books, fascinated with every entry that had the Fields name on it. March 29, 1933: Thomas Walter to Rebekah four acres for "the love and affection that I have for my wife, Rebekah Elizabeth." But I could not find my grandfather's will. Neither could I find a deed for land transferred to Simon Toombs.

I stuck my head in the door of Pat's office.

"I'm off to North Carolina. Thank you for your help. I may need to call you from home."

"Wait, Molly. I have a feeling you need to talk to B. B. Rogers. She's the local matriarch, knows everybody, quite wealthy. Let me call her for you."

Mrs. Rogers was home and invited me right over. She lived in an attractive one-level brick house nestled in a copse of trees that were surrounded by acres of cotton. I was taken by the genteel mannerisms of this petite, graying, white and southern lady.

She offered me a Coke and led me into the large den. I took a moment to absorb the colors in the chintz fabric and the appealing pieces of folk art scattered about the room.

After we chatted about her experience learning to farm after her husband died, we went through the family tree. Her mother and Mamaw were bridge buddies. She remembered playing bridge with my parents and other young couples before Dad left the Delta. I had a sense that this gracious woman would be guarded. When she told me she recently received a letter from her good friend, Aunt Sis, I knew I needed to parse my words.

"Mrs. Rogers, can you tell me anything about the shooting of two black men in 1946? My father was charged."

She sat up a bit taller and her jaw stiffened.

"I don't remember very much about that. I'm not real sure what happened. We were so worried about your daddy. He was so talented, had such a wonderful gift with words."

I questioned whether I should drop the subject but stepped off the cliff.

"Many people I've talked to say that Uncle Bill was responsible for the deaths, not my father."

She repositioned herself on the sofa. "It was just such a horrible thing. We all just tried to push it aside."

Instead of pressing forward I decided to let silence have its way. When the stillness became unbearable, she said, "Well, all I can tell you, Molly, is that your uncle Bill was hotheaded. He was less able to accept the changes that were coming to the Delta, and he was very young."

There was a finality to her statement that let me know our conversation was over. I didn't have the courage to tell her about the possibility that my father had shot his own half-brother. The notion was rattling around in my head. But on some level I knew that this might be the closest I would come to knowing the truth about the gunman.

She offered to drive me around Anguilla, and we stopped at Ashland Plantation where only a brick chimney stood as a landmark of the former family home. We drove past other familial sites, and she told me a story about Mamaw. Seems that she went to Memphis with two friends to shop and stay at the Peabody Hotel. They went to a movie late in the afternoon. Mamaw took off her shoes. Her feet and ankles began to swell so that her shoes no longer fit. B. B. laughed when she told me that Mamaw had to walk barefoot into the lobby of the Peabody.

Maybe it was the heat of the afternoon or the comfort of being B. B.'s passenger or the sound of the tires on dirt and gravel roads, but fatigue was getting the best of me. I thanked B. B. for our time together and left for Yazoo City.

The next day I left Anguilla with more questions than answers. It seemed important to drive to Vicksburg before turning east. I thought that if I made a personal appearance at the Warren County Courthouse, I might be able to gain access to the files of the district attorney who charged Dad with manslaughter. The clerk introduced me to the current district attorney, and he told me that T. J. Lawrence's files were nowhere to be found. Computer records in their office did not go back as far as 1946. I was disappointed but not surprised. The hour-long drive to one of the South's most historic cities, however, was well worth the time. The Mississippi River flows along steep embankments above which the carefully restored nineteenth-century inner city proudly rests. I thought about being born in a place so thoroughly steeped in the aura of Civil War bloodshed. The brutality of that war and the world wars had to scar the minds of soldiers just as it had the land. I wondered, would Dad have been so quick to fire the gun if he hadn't seen combat? But then, what would have provoked Uncle Bill, who did not serve overseas, to shoot two men? He was only twenty years old.

☙❧

The next morning, while driving east through the north Georgia mountains, my mind drifted back. I remembered a family gathering in North Carolina when I was eleven or twelve. Mamaw summoned the entire family to the rustic High Hampton Inn in Cashiers. The bark-sided lodge was situated amid tall pine trees in front of a deep lake. Chimney Mountain filled the backdrop rising from the far shore. After a delicious supper served family-style in the dining room, my father took Mamaw's arm, and escorted her out the front door and across the covered front porch where "old" people rocked and talked. I followed behind and stifled a gasp when the elastic waistband of Mamaw's silk boxer underpants gave way. They dropped to her feet. Without hesitation, without a change in expression, without pausing in conversation, she quietly stopped, reached to the floor, whisked her panties off the ground, and stuffed them in her pocketbook. The rockers began to twitter and giggle. My face turned scarlet but we continued to saunter across the porch and off to our cabin.

In 1984, when Mamaw died, family members descended on Anguilla like homing pigeons. The night before her funeral, twelve of her adult grandchildren gathered in the den at Uncle Bill and Aunt Lib's house after supper. We had our own private wake; memories surfaced. We laughed and we cried. I told the underpants story.

CHAPTER ELEVEN

Silencing of a Community

July 2006

Both black people and white people in the Deep South were so fearful of each other, so intimidated by the potential for power struggles to erupt into violence, that the safety they found in their own numbers contributed to a hardened code of silence. My family began to suppress the truth the moment it became known. Mr. Evans told me that the black community shut down for days, fearful to mention the shootings to one another. Even on the plantations, the races may have worked side by side and interacted freely in the course of a day's work, but they kept their business to themselves. Gathering together took place on Sundays at church where, after the service, black families shared a meal, talked shop, gossiped while the children played games in the churchyard. Then and even now, churches were the social hubs of rural black life.

When I returned to Asheville, I was plagued by a sense of loss—that had Simon survived, I might have had a chance to meet and know a third uncle. He was a good man, according to his family, affable and, I gather, somewhat charismatic. We might have shared common interests and the tender connection of blood relatives. Trying to imagine what his funeral was like, I read the book *Passed On: African American Mourning Stories* by Karla Holloway.

From her research I put together a picture of what might have happened after Simon and David were shot. First, their bodies would have been taken to the homes of their mothers for a wake or "settin' up" because it was important for families and friends to see the dead men for the last time. Churchwomen would bring in food—fried chicken, turnip greens, sweet potato pie, cake. Later, because there was seldom a way to embalm the body, black morticians would take it "out to the garage, place him on a couple of straight boards and wrap him in muslin. Then, we packed newspapers into the pine coffins that we put together and buried him without further ado—it only cost us about fifty dollars." Sometimes the bottoms of the coffins were hinged so that the body could be dropped into the grave and the casket reused. The burials would have occurred before the funerals took place, Simon's at Southdale Missionary Baptist Church.

On Sunday, when workers were free to go to church, they would have gathered together. Inez and Rose and their father and mother, along with Simon's mother, would hear a cathartic sermon rousing the congregation to lament the loss of two young men to white aggression. There would have been movement, dramatic gesturing, speeches, and songs. And the minister might have taken the opportunity to incite the congregation to have hope, not to give up because the world in which they lived was full of evil. He promised them they would see a better place in heaven.

In a letter from King Evans dated May 31, 2006, he wrote, "Negroes survived in this country because of a deep and abiding faith in God. We believe the scriptures and know that, 'Vengeance is Mine, saith the Lord' and that someday they will face the righteous judge and will get His reward. This belief is true for the black person who feels that God will justly reward him for his obedience and the white man for his treatment of blacks. Unfortunately, our government and laws supported this system that made it lawful to mistreat fellow human beings."

After the service, there would have been talk about what happened. Rumors and angry words would not move outside the community there. It is quite possible that a traveling minstrel, like Muddy Waters, who lived in Rolling Fork, might have stopped by at the end of the day and struck up a bluesy tune or two. When all returned to their plantation homes and prepared to resume their work in a new week, the story would not be talked about again.

At my grandmother's home, silence about the incident took another form. After Dr. Goodman came to the house to see Tom and bind his wound, and after Sheriff Crawford took Dad into custody, the family probably framed a story they could live with, attributing the killings to self-defense. Quite possibly, that was all there was to it. Mamaw gave the sheriff five thousand dollars for bond. She would have tried to shield my mother by making light of what happened, telling her of only one death. Bill and Tom might have spoken about the "nigrahs" who died, but only in anger for the distress they had caused. And Sis finished out her holiday vacation from school, attending as many parties as the Delta had to offer. As soon as Dad was free to go home, two days after the incident, he returned to his family and his desk at the *Pilot*. What actually happened was closeted, denied, rationalized, justified, and pushed aside. Since Dad was not going to be held accountable, there was no reason to belabor a bad situation.

My mother corresponded with her parents through letter writing. I found one of those letters dated July 5, 1947, a mere six months after that gray December day. In her beautiful script, she wrote:

Dearest Folks,

So much has been happening! We went to Vicksburg to a big celebration. General Eisenhower made a wonderful speech—but the most wonderful part of all—Jay got to meet him due to his owning a newspaper, and his influence with his fellow pressmen. We sat on the platform with him, and I had the supreme pleasure of flipping a bug off of his shoulder!! I was standing behind him when a picture was taken and "Ike" and I were on the front page of the *Commercial Appeal* to-day! It was purely accidental, but boy, do I feel important!! We got home from Vicksburg around 3 o'clock and our whole crowd had a picnic out on the bayou near Alice's house. I have never seen so much food in all my life— I'm still full!! All in all we had a grand 4th of July. When we got home the baby was asleep and so was Minnie!

In the same carefree voice, she wrote about her baby boy with words of pride and pleasure. Then she signed it, "We love you, Jay, Jaybo, and Betsy." Later, I found out that she spent the rest of that summer in Bristol with her parents, "avoiding the heat."

Though life resumed for my family, and the "unfortunate" event faded into the background, I had a strong feeling that because family members were so protective of the secret sixty years later, there had to have been more to it. I called a cousin of my father in Anguilla. She lived on the same stretch of Highway 61 that Mamaw did and they were very close. With care yet hopeful, I approached the subject with her. She begged me not to look any further into the incident. She said, "Molly, this is an uncertain world. I don't want this to be talked around. As a parent, I'm suggesting that you be very careful. Both Jay and Bill are gone. Don't dig into this. It could be heartbreaking for you. If this gets in print, it could be very bad. Settle yourself. I am thinking of only one person when I say this and that is you." I slumped in my chair and placed the receiver in its cradle.

ᙍᔥᙓ

After my trip to Anguilla, I contacted Pat Thrasher at the Sharkey County Courthouse. I asked if Dr. Goodman's or Sheriff Crawford's records had been filed away somewhere. She said that they had been burned. I also asked if death certificates might be available. "No" was her answer but she referred me to the current coroner, Olamae Holmes, who verified Pat's account. It was apparent that the paper trail had become weedy and only led into a deep thicket of confusion.

I resorted to my box of papers collected over the years. I recovered a newspaper article written about my grandmother before she died. I found out what was keeping her busy during the war years when her sons were off fighting. When the government began controlling the number of acres that could be devoted to cotton planting, she became aware that many of the women living on the plantation were no longer needed as field hands. "Miss Rebecca" devised a scheme that started with a trip to Dalton, Georgia, where she learned how to make chenille bedspreads by a process called "big dotting." When she returned home with supplies in hand, she packaged the materials needed and handed them out to those who were willing to learn how to sew. She set up a workspace where they made over five hundred quilts, and Mamaw took them to individual department stores, Neiman Marcus in Dallas, Maison Blanche in New Orleans, and Goldsmiths in Memphis. She even sent one to Eleanor Roosevelt in 1934, while FDR was still in the White House. The bedspreads were adorned with a label which read, "Mammy Made with Plantation Aid." Unfortunately, Congress enacted the Wage and Hour Law about that time. Because piecework would force her to pay an hourly wage, Mamaw felt she had to shut down her business.

King Evans responded to my concerns about how Mamaw handled the shooting incident by saying,

> I, too, believe that your grandmother, Ms. Rebecca, was devastated by the incident. She was concerned about the tenants on Ashland Plantation. I recall one instance where she had an entire seed house converted to accommodate a chenille bedspread sewing operation to provide employment for black women. Mrs. Hattie Martin would dress up as "Aunt Jemima" and sell the spreads to people as they stopped at the gas station. This appeared to be a profitable business until eastern imports undersold everybody. A painting of the seed house was hanging in the Fields Planting Office.

My aunts and uncles told me that Mamaw was featured in *National Geographic* in the '40s. When I went to Pack Library in downtown Asheville and asked to see the volumes from that time I found in the February 1941 issue a lengthy article on cotton. Included was a photograph of Mamaw's gin in Anguilla. It showed field hands resting atop rectangular bales of cotton. Horse-drawn wagons loaded with cotton filled the yard, each painted a different pastel color. That was part of the system to keep up with the various plantations' pickin's. The following words appear beneath the picture: "'Gin' originally was born—a contraction of the drawling negro pronunciation of 'engine.'"

Family lore has it that one year during harvest time, Mamaw drove all night to Arkansas to pick up a part for a broken machine at the gin. She returned just at daybreak the next morning—in time for the work that lay ahead. She was a force. And I struggled with the certainty that my writing about Dad, Bill, and Tom would make her very unhappy. There would be no way for me to pursue this story were she still alive. I would not forsake her love. She was even more entrenched in a time period, in a racial stance that set her apart, that was her means of survival, that defined her, than my father's generation. Her reactions to her life experiences were preconditioned and subconscious. Though I would love to converse with her about the subtle forms of racism that exist today, she would find it difficult to relate to my experience. The "best" of Mamaw was her intense love of family, her loyalty to her children, and the grandeur of her spirit. She would fold but she would not crumble.

⚶

In the summer of 2006, I discovered a small Cape Cod for sale at the end of a cul-de-sac right down the street from my writer friend, Glenda. It perched just above the Swannanoa River and had flooded during Ivan and Katrina—forty-four inches of water filled the first floor of the house. By 2006, the owner, tired of making things right, put his place on the market. I knew a blessing when I saw one, and two things sealed the deal—one was a second-story bedroom with double-hung windows that gave me a view of the woods beyond the river. It was the perfect place for my desk and computer. But the Swannanoa itself grabbed my heart at first glance. About fifty yards from the back door I could put my toe into the gurgling, sparkling, cool mountain runoff that would flow through my days and lull me to sleep at night.

At first, I didn't make the connection to family history. Not ten miles upriver, my great-grandparents (on Mamaw's side) had owned a rambling country boardinghouse that had been a sanitarium. They called it the Riverby Inn. When the Delta summer heat percolated up into misery, and mosquitoes were breeding in the swamps, my grandfather Thomas loaded Mamaw and all four kids into their big black Buick and sent them to North Carolina. In the years prior to his death, he joined them there. The inn became a nest of busy activity when cousins, aunts, and uncles converged. The children were conscripted into the garden brigade. There were plenty of other chores too.

Dad, as oldest grandchild, was responsible for herding the children out of sight when a prospective overnighter pulled into the gravel driveway. The mountain air was both a balm and an energizer. The kids played hard, created adventures, and "walked the pipe." Below the house, where the Swannanoa lay in its bed, a large pipe connected the shore to an island. To pass muster and prove not to be a baby, the boys walked the pipe—gingerly placing one foot in front of the other, trying not to fall prey to the taunts and jeers of the ones who made it across and trying not to fall into the chilly mountain water. Sis recounted in her homemade book, a collection of stories about the Riverby, that she was sometimes carried across by Uncle Leon. To hell with muster. She just wanted to be with the boys.

So now I live downstream of the happy days of my dad and his siblings. I can feel the delight, the false bravado and the scheming of the kids, the loving arms of grandparents, and the thrill of natural beauty waft over me on the summer breeze. I am bound by water, by blood, to this lineage, to people who could forget about the dark corners in their hearts when they left the Delta for high ground.

October 11, 2006

Asheville's mountainscape could not be prettier than in the fall when the leaves turn myriad shades of red, gold and, brown. It isn't unusual to wake up to see pockets of mist rising from the coves.

One crisp morning I phoned Mom. It seemed like a good idea to let her know what I was up to. She asked what was going on with me, and I explained that I was working on the 1946 story and had writer's block. I had, I thought, exhausted all sources and hoped she would help me out.

"The last time we spoke about this, Molly, was very upsetting to me. I don't want to go into any depth. I just don't feel like it."

I assured her that she didn't have to talk further if it was too painful.

"Go ahead."

First I told her that I had driven to Mississippi twice and interviewed a witness and several family members of one of the dead men.

"You're kidding. Why does this fascinate you so much?"

I explained that I was learning about Dad—who he was and why he acted as he did and that somehow I hoped it would help me to understand myself a bit better.

"Uh-huh." I detected a note of sarcasm in her voice.

"Well, I felt that as a mother, and I think most mothers try to shelter their children whether it's to their benefit or not . . . I should keep this to myself."

She asked if I had talked to Hodding Carter. I explained that both he and Betty were no longer alive. I didn't bother to tell her that I had contacted, with no success, the library where his papers were filed. Neither did she need to know that I had e-mailed his son Hodding, who is the University Professor of Leadership and Public Policy at UNC–Chapel Hill. He responded, "I'm sorry to say I know nothing of the incident, though I'm sure that black folks had a different interpretation of events. Good luck in your search. It is the kind of story that most white Mississippians prefer to bury—but so do most people everywhere."

Knowing that Mom had such a strong desire to bury the story, I continued with trepidation. I took a deep breath and told her that there were opposing stories about who pulled the trigger. And I explained that there might have been further motivation for Dad, Bill, and Tom to go to the juke joint that night. It might be true that Simon was Dad's half-brother with land deeded to him.

"I did not know that," she said in a flat, unemotional tone. "I know nothing about it. I frankly did not want to go into it." That statement indicated to me that she had been privy to conversations at the time of the murders but made a conscious decision to stay in the dark.

Then Mom took the reins. "Have you told your sister about this?"

I told Mom that because of her reticence to talk about the subject, I hadn't broached it with Laura. I just didn't think it was my place to bring it up.

"That's nice. I see no reason to. She has nice memories of her father in my opinion, why disturb her with it." *What was Mom thinking? Laura dealt with Dad's drinking by refusing to allow him to come to her house. She was very protective of her small children. Her hard stand with Dad was a healthy decision, but it effectively ended her relationship with him.*

We talked in a lighthearted vein for a few minutes before I asked her why Dad hadn't become a farmer.

"He knew as much about farming as he knew about . . . I always said that he should have stayed in the service. He was good at it. He was respected. He had friends. Of course, he was not drinkin' as much then. That's just my opinion. He had to do his own thing."

Then I told her about Dad's family's reluctance to talk to me about what happened. Even Myrtis Greer, Dad's cousin, had admonished me to stay away from "this."

"Mom, what could break my heart that I don't already know?"

I could sense that she was retracting from the conversation. She told me she didn't have anything more to say about what happened. She reiterated her concern that I found the incident so fascinating and she said, "Frankly, I don't think you ought to dig into it either."

My feeble attempt to explain myself came out like this. "Well, the thing is, Mom, you lived through the horror of it. I didn't. I don't have the same emotional feelings about it, but I truly don't want to do anything that would hurt you."

Seamlessly she changed the topic and began to talk about her death. She told me that she just wanted to go in peace. She just wanted to die quietly and without anger. After we got off the line, I puzzled over those words. *Mom is going to be hesitant to talk to me about anything now.* She doesn't trust me. And maybe, there is more to be revealed.

CHAPTER TWELVE

Obstacles

December 2006

I'd spent the fall studying the family tree, sifting through photographs, poring over my notes. I could accept, intellectually, that Dad walked into a quagmire when he and Mom moved to the Delta after the war. He encountered opposition at the Pan Am that night, physical aggression that sparked into a fistfight and David Jones's drawing his pistol—all of which he may have thought he could handle sanely and maturely, but if he drew a gun and began to fire it, some stress point in him must have been triggered. Or instinct took over. When that happened, the aftereffects of his war experience may have caused him to dissociate as any veteran suffering from "shell shock" would have done. Since the Vietnam War, we have known the psychological effects of battle fatigue. Dad could have had remnants of those symptoms less than two years after his service. His sense of safety had been compromised; he was accustomed to being hypervigilant; he may have been self-medicating with alcohol to quell the anxiety that war service had instilled in him. When Dad, Bill, and Tom entered the scene, verbal aggression gave way to physical aggression so Dad may have broken a sweat, tensed his muscles, experienced a pounding heart. And with his training, he would have had a sensitive trigger finger and rapid response reaction. But even this scenario was hard for me to assimilate. Later, my cousin Tommy told me that his father took the first bullet—the one that landed in Tom's shoulder. Maybe Dad was acting in self-defense at that point and protecting himself, Bill, and Tom from further harm. After all, Tommy had also said, "Jay saved my dad's life."

What about Simon? Rumor had it that he was sitting on the front porch of the station. If Inez and Rose were correct and his wounds entered from the back, and if King Evans's story was correct—that Simon was lying on the ground when he arrived on the scene, minutes after the gunfire—then Dad or Bill would have shot him in the back as he attempted to get away. That, certainly, would have been a homicide.

I stayed in contact with Inez and Carolyn Hackett, King Evans's daughter. More names surfaced. More rumors surfaced. There must have been a buzz in the community after I took the lid off of the beehive. Someone told Inez that the Fields men went to the station to find Simon to get him to pick up a black woman in Hollandale for their pleasure. That rumor was more than I wanted to think about. My mode of denying myself the truth—then and now—was to obfuscate. Information cut loose and sought different ports in my brain so all I could do was shut down and discount stories I couldn't fit neatly into my mental picture—the one I could live with.

Inez suggested that I go see the nurse of Dr. Goodman, who pronounced Simon and David dead. He had been a friend of the family. I began to feel a nudge to go back and sort some of this out. And then it dawned on me that December was approaching. I could be in Anguilla on the twelfth, the sixtieth anniversary of the shootings.

On December 11, I made the long drive to Anguilla once again. My first stop was at the home of Carabelle Johnson, Dr. Goodman's black nurse. She lived two houses down the street from King Evans. The stooped, smiling woman met me at the door, walker in hands, wearing a deep blue housecoat and tired slippers.

We sat across her dining table, and she began by talking about how she went to work to help support her mother and her own fatherless child. "Dr. Goodman," she said, "was the best white person you ever seen in your life." He was the only doctor in Anguilla at the time so he was glad to have Carabelle's help. His wife taught her to use a syringe by showing her how to draw up water and then shoot it into an orange. Carabelle left home for Memphis, where she studied nursing and became an R. N. "I wanted to do the best I can in life."

I asked her about the shooting.

"The next morning I went on to work as I usually do. People were standing around and whispering, but I don't know what they were talking about. There were rumors—that Mr. H. J. had killed two men up at Anguilla. There were a lot of rumors. You know how things are. Anyway, Dr. Goodman asked me why [it happened] and I said, I don't know, Doctor, and I didn't know."

When I asked her if she believed the rumor that my father was not the gunman, she said, "It was rumored that Mr. Bill had the gun. It was sure rumored. That it wasn't your daddy that did it."

I left Carabelle's house feeling frustrated and defeated even though she shared some wonderful stories with me about my grandmother. Then I drove out to Ashland to look for the cemetery that Uncle Bill provided for the black community. I didn't find it. When I drove across the Deer Creek, slowly taking in the scene of cypress trees dripping with Spanish moss and exposed roots that sought the silt at the bottom of the creek, I remembered sitting on the bridge with my father, casting fishing line from bamboo poles into the brackish water. I was an impatient child, not cut out for waiting around on fish all afternoon. But my dad, always full of stories, held me spellbound for long periods in the late evening sun.

Driving toward Rolling Fork, I realized that as hard as I searched to find out my father's role in the killings, I might not be able to get at the truth. Dad, Tom, and Bill went to the Pan Am station as a united front—a brotherhood, fueled by alcohol, energized by zealous power, racial bias, and entitlement. I had spoken with enough people in the Delta to know that there was a clear divide in perception. Most whites believed that Dad was the primary perpetrator; it was reported in the newspapers that way. Most blacks believed that Uncle Bill was responsible for the deaths. The rumors were abundant and too hard to verify. Too many knowledgeable people were dead now. I had to make choices about who to believe and how far to go in search of the truth. I gave myself permission to trust my own discernment, but my judgment was tarnished by a need to believe that Dad didn't have it in him to shoot with the intent to kill, and further to believe that if he had done so, he would have felt crippling remorse for it. In the months ahead, I was going to have to try and tease out Dad's moral compass from the prevailing mores of the south Delta culture of the 1940s.

❧

I stopped by the office of the *Deer Creek Pilot* just to schmooze Ray Mosby and see if he had anything else to say, though when I first entered the door I got a "here she comes again" look. I read Dad's editorials one more time, noting the predominance of space dedicated to alcohol. In January 1949, eleven days after I was born, Dad wrote, "Should Mississippi's legislators recognize the eminent threat to our economic and emotional security presented by the alcoholic, it is highly doubtful that the state would be in a position to do other than recognize the danger. As a 'dry' state, whiskey swilling Mississippi gets an infinitesimal portion of the tremendous profits made by dealers in what has become a staple commodity."

Then Ray moseyed into the conference room where I sat. In past conversations, he waxed poetic about his territory and about the newspaper business. But this time, he questioned what I was really up to. When I told him, he stroked his unshaven chin and said he guessed that Dad was able to walk away from punishment and retribution because he was the older son, the "scion" of the family. He gained notoriety because of what he had done. "He was someone not to mess with." I wondered how Dad held up under that much pretense and bravado. For the life of me, I couldn't see Dad carrying out such a heavy role, at least not after the night gunfire broke out at the Pan Am. Maybe, after all was said and done, he felt no remorse. Maybe he was so steeped in the myth of white supremacy that he felt justified in taking two lives, firing three or four bullets into the body of one of them.

Ray told me to track down Charles Weissinger, the county attorney. "He's the local historian, he'll know more," he said. I shelved that idea for the rest of the day and returned to Yazoo to regroup.

The next morning, I woke knowing that Weissinger had some answers I needed. I drove over to Rolling Fork and stopped at his office before I did anything else. As I was getting out of the car, a middle-aged man came out of the office building, into the parking lot. He was graying at the temples, had a prominent mustache, and wore glasses, a dress shirt, and tie.

"I'm looking for Charles Weissinger." He smiled at this so I introduced myself and asked if we could talk.

At first, he disclaimed that he was the local historian. He was from Cary, Mississippi, and his interests were in the pre–Civil War times. But he suggested that we go to the courthouse. He might be able to show me something there, a deed issued to a black man for land on my grandfather's Ashland Plantation. While he studied maps and looked through deed books, I talked to him about my research and the stories I'd been told. When I told him that the killings were related to the unlawful sale of alcohol, he stopped his research and turned to face me.

"No. Those men died because of land. Simon was your father's brother. It all had to do with land."

But Charles wasn't able to locate the deed. I felt impatient with him for being so adamant about the story he told. If he was so sure, why couldn't he prove it to me? Maybe my anger was a way of deflecting what I really felt—frustrated, tired, defeated. I knew

Charles's time was valuable, so after an hour or so, when he told me he needed to get back to his office, I prepared to take my leave. But before we parted he said, "You need to talk to some of the black Fields." I filed that away, uncertain that I had the nerve to follow through. At that time, the voices of my aunts and cousins spoke loudest in my head. "Don't go there, Molly. Leave it alone. You will destroy our reputation for no good reason." I deferred. I had a reputation too. Anyway, it was an important day, the anniversary of Simon's and David's deaths, and I had an appointment to go see the Evans family again.

Mr. Evans looked paler and thinner than on the last visit. He was quieter, too. When we were alone in the living room, Carolyn told me that he had been diagnosed with colon cancer. She didn't know how long her father would be alive.

"Carolyn, I want to ask a favor of you and hope that you will tell me if you are not comfortable with it." She nodded. "Today is the sixtieth anniversary of the shootings. Would you be willing to go to the Pan Am station with me to take my picture there?"

"I don't have a problem with that."

I asked if her father would like to ride in the car with us. She, her mother, and King, Jr., helped him into the front seat. I sat behind him.

"That's the old storage house for the soybeans," King said. "That's the land Mr. Vick used to own. You know, they named the city of Vicksburg after him." We drove and talked and laughed. Then we parked across the street from the deteriorating gray gas station that once housed a saloon for "coloreds."

I took my position in front of the boarded-up windows, and while Carolyn framed her shots—walking back and forth to the car to check on her father—I tried to imagine my grandmother's car rolling to an abrupt stop in front of the station. I envisioned Dad, Bill, and Tom entering the building and hustling into the back room where the black men were seated, drinking. In my mind, a brawl broke out, heated up, and combusted into open fire. In the gunsmoke-filled room, I saw David lying in his own blood, Tom faltering, the other blacks scurrying out of the building followed by Dad or Bill with pistol aimed in front. I saw Simon on the ground between me and the Evans's Buick. The scene took shape like a movie, but I was only a bystander consumed by the moment, shocked and outraged. My father crossed a line with fatal consequences. That similar deeds took place frequently during those days did not soften the horror I felt. In that moment of heightened awareness, I had an epiphany. If I kept this story to myself, I would be joining in the conspiracy of my family and the deceit of many white Americans. The more time I spent with the black members of this community, the more tenuous was the Fields grip on my throat.

We returned to King's house and helped him back into his recliner. Carolyn and I talked again about the painful days ahead for her family. She had mixed emotions about accepting her father's wish to let his life end without further efforts to extend it. I told her about my job with hospice and how important it is to walk beside the person who is doing the difficult work of dying. We talked in hushed voices, our heads close together, like sisters. Before I left, she said, "Girl, you better stay in touch."

After I left the Evans family, I was struck by the irony of being a guest in their home, a passenger in their car. And I marveled at the significance of having Carolyn, a black resident of Anguilla, take my picture at the scene where my father or his brother had killed two black men.

❧

At four o'clock that afternoon, I went to Mamaw's house to meet the present owner. She was gracious and gave me free rein to explore on my own. It saddened me that the stately brick home, so full of good memories, was no longer part of the family. The living room was not as large as I remembered it as a child. The new owner had painted the walls Chinese red, but the mantel and bookcases were still a crisp white. The hardwood floors were bare except for a smattering of oriental throw rugs. I saw my grandmother in every room. She sat in the sunroom, sewing; on the side porch, eating cantelope at the glass-top table under a whirring ceiling fan; in the kitchen, handing off a pot roast to Aunt Mat who set it in the oven. I saw her in her bedroom, piled up in a bevy of feather pillows with her Bible and the *Ladies' Home Journal*.

I remembered a story Dad told me. In 1927, when he was six and in the first grade in the tiny elementary school in Anguilla, Mamaw noticed that the poor white children from Sunflower River were coming to school in the fall, many barefooted, some with their long johns sewn so as not to be removed until spring. Every day, they carried small tin pails with the same lunch: molasses and biscuits. Mamaw read in the *Good Housekeeping Magazine* that it was safe to can meat. Dad wrote about it:

> First, she asked Dad for one of the slaughter heifers he was carefully corning out for our own winter's beef supply. She did the same thing of Billy McKinney and M. C. Ewing, and they too found her appeal irresistible. Next she organized a crew—only the most experienced men to slaughter and butcher the animals, and women cooks borrowed from the kitchens of homes known for the quality of their tables, who would simmer the beef and rich stock adhering strictly to the *Good Houskeeping* instructions.
>
> The men had come in the early morning cool, and by the time we arrived, three carcasses hung from the limbs of a giant oak tree in one corner of the school yard, and kerosene stoves burbled on the bare concrete floor of the "kitchen." The men had knocked together crude tables from planks they had brought from home, and there soon began the succession of butchering, simmering and canning the beef and broth in gallon cans which had to be specially ordered from Gibb's store. The activity occupied the entire long summer Saturday.
>
> When it was through, the neat, shiny cans of beef in rich broth lined the shelves of a storeroom which the school principal had devoted to the project. Mother had a stout

padlock installed on the door, and she dropped both keys into her purse.

The cache went untouched during the warm months of September and October, while Mother organized the final phase of her project, the recruitment of responsible serving crews for the winter months.

Then, each noon during the school week, that meat and stock, augmented by vegetables as they were available, became piping hot soups, stews, ragouts and hash for any child who would come, but not including Tom, Bill and me nor any of our schoolmates whose parents could provide hot lunches at home.

Mother's late summer project was continued for several years, ending only when the state instituted its school lunch program.

Mother had not been able to wait for that!

At Mamaw's, I discovered the back stairwell that led from the second floor directly into the kitchen. I could see my father and his brothers scurrying up the lofty incline of the steps playing games of hide-and-seek or just managing to get out of Mamaw's reach. And though the kitchen had been thoroughly modernized, I could still see Aunt Mat sitting in a cane-bottomed chair in the corner, issuing directives to the Fields children who were her charge.

A flood of pleasant memories filled me when I walked into the breakfast room. It had booth seats beside the window and a floor-to-ceiling wood cabinet painted white with glass doors on top. In the center was a counter where there was always a large round red tin of fresh sugar and thumbprint cookies. I wondered if Mamaw caught Dad's hand in that tin one time too many.

The pleasure of being in my grandmother's home didn't vanish until I was back in my car, leaving Anguilla. A lump in my throat and an attempt to fight back tears settled on me as I drove away. Mamaw knew how hard it was for me at home. She knew that Mom was a high-maintenance woman who loved her children but could not show it. She knew that Dad would never measure

up to the high financial standards that Mother's parents maintained. She knew that I was buffeted about by my parents' marital discord. Because of that, she wrote me letters on powder-blue
stationery that arrived at our house at least once a month. Her
backhand, lefty scrawl was unmistakable. Sometimes she called
just to see how I was doing. When we were together, her feath-
erbed body enfolded me and I knew beyond any doubt what love
looked and felt like. I had a strong sense that I was her favorite
grandchild, but my cousins probably felt that way too. She had a
way of making all of us feel special.

This trip to Mississippi provided a detailed re-creation of the
lowest point of my father's life. My understanding of the role he
played in the death of Simon and David had only grown more
vivid and honed because of a deeper feel for the Old South, its
ways and its tragic inability to overcome economic, social, and,
especially, racial divides. My journey was rife with nostalgia. Yes,
my connection to the place had grown thin and shallow over time,
but love for it still danced in my heart.

⁂

Back in Asheville, I sifted through the mail and found a Christmas card from Aunt Sis. She wrote, "I must admit—I was somewhat tweaked that you could not come to Tom's funeral yet within
weeks you made a trip all the way to Mississippi on a wild goose
trail." I let those angry words flow through me knowing that I
would hear them again.

CHAPTER THIRTEEN

Breakdown

January 2007

When I spoke to Charles Weissinger, the attorney in Rolling Fork, he suggested that Fielding Wright might have represented my father before the grand jury. In 1939, Wright left his law firm to become governor of Mississippi and moved to Vicksburg. After the shootings, Dad was immersed in newspaper work. He was chairman of the Press-Radio Committee of the Delta Council, wrote articles for *South Magazine* and several major southern newspapers. He covered the Democratic National Convention in Philadelphia in 1947 for the *Vicksburg Post-Herald* and became a member of Fielding Wright's staff. Charles thought Wright's papers might still be boxed at the Jackson or Vicksburg offices where he last practiced law. I called Granville Tate at the Brunini law firm in Jackson. Nothing surfaced, but Granville did offer to help me find an abstractor who would investigate land records for a deed at the Sharkey County Courthouse.

❧

As my family's first summer in Bristol wore on, Mom bought a used pool table and had it moved into the basement game room. Jay made friends with the neighborhood boys and they gravitated to our house to play pool, listen to Jay's collection of 45 records, all beach music and jazz, and they practiced swearing. The poolroom was a magnet for boys from both sides of the tracks—much to Mom's chagrin. There were, however, no blacks stopping by for an afternoon of brotherhood.

In the low light of the basement room, after football practice, Jay's friends stretched their lanky bodies across the green felt, banking shots, putting a little English into the stroke of the cue stick, sometimes sinking a ball with a fast direct hit. The next player stood ready, chalking the tip of his stick.

Every now and then I snuck downstairs, sidling into the shadows to watch and listen. I loved the smell of sweaty boys fresh from football practice. Firm muscles were outlined under their white tee shirts, and the crack of the cue ball breaking open the game sent a shiver down my spine.

Occasionally, Eddie Childs walked by and tousled my hair or poked at me with his cue stick. The sleeve of his shirt was always turned up to enfold a pack of Camels. Eddie, who was nineteen in the tenth grade, had a James Dean swagger.

I felt like a little sister to some of the boys. More than anything, I wanted to belong to my brother's group of friends. Normalcy had to look like this. And after carefully observing the game, I started practicing on the sly. I figured out something that I thought few girls my age would know: some pool strokes required finesse.

The boys' language thrilled me even though I didn't know the meaning of some of the words.

"Frank, you fucking nerd. You're playing the stripes, not the solids."

"Eddie, how 'bout goin down to 'Courtesy' and pickin' up a coupla six packs."

"Would everybody please just shut the fuck up so I can concentrate here?"

One afternoon, Jay borrowed his friend's baby-blue Ford convertible and took off for Hills Department Store. While Jay was in the store, another friend started the car, revved up the engine, turned the wheel as far to the left as it would go and stepped on the gas. Customers returning to the parking lot went back inside the store while they watched the Ford do tight 360 degree circles. Someone called the cops.

Meanwhile, Jay finished purchasing a dartboard for the pool-room and returned to the now docile car, which he admitted was a lot more powerful machine than he had ever driven before. On his way back to Long Crescent, he crested the hill beside Sullins College at 65 mph and came to a screeching, rubber-laying halt at the intersection at the foot of the hill where four squad cars waited. He barely missed them.

Standing before the judge, he said, "Your honor, that car was just too fast for me."

At home that night anger flared between Mom and Dad when they couldn't agree on a proper punishment, and I swore to myself I was not going down the road that Jay was on. After supper, while discussing how he planned to get out to the country club to play golf without a driver's license, Jay finally broke down and apologized, but he still had to walk the eight miles to the course.

"Mom, I'm sorry. I just couldn't tell on my friends." After that escapade and several others, I saw cracks in Mom's cool, sophisticated veneer. Eventually, she caved in and gave Jay his driving privileges.

❧

On my fifteenth birthday, in January 1964, Mom hired a police officer to teach me how to drive. She said she was too nervous to do it herself. There was a tremor in her hands, and she startled when I came into a room too fast. Officer Broom was not young or handsome but after several Saturdays behind the wheel of Mom's brown Bel Air, he was looking good to me. I thought he might marry me and get me out of the house.

My friend and next-door neighbor, Lynn, and I occasionally managed to convince one or the other of our mothers that she needed something at the grocery so that we could get one of the family cars and scoot out of the neighborhood. I loved it when Mary V. let us drive her Nash Rambler because it was small and I thought virtually unnoticeable, when in truth it was a hiccup of a vehicle that forever held up traffic because even when floored, it would only just break 45. It helped that cocktail hour started at 5:00 and our parents forgot that we were out in the car. That way we could make a grocery run last a good hour.

Though the Kroger was due east and only a few blocks from home, we made a beeline north to the high school to circle the practice field where the football team worked out. Lynn knew the numbered jerseys by heart. I had a crush on number 12, and she had the hots for number 42. Of course they were seniors and above paying attention to two underclassmen. Nonetheless, it seemed as if every time we made the circuit, one of those numbers turned to look and I doubled over so as not to be seen while Lynn floored the gas pedal.

We didn't miss a football game that year and though we tried our damndest to bring the home team to victory by the sheer force of our screaming voices, our school lost the big rivalry game to Tennessee High. It was a crushing blow, and I felt bad for Jay, even though he didn't get off the bench all season.

The following spring Mom and Dad invited the Goodpastures to go to Florida with them to spend a week at Mam and Joe's house in Delray. The night before they left, Mom said, "Jay and Molly, you are old enough to stay at home by yourselves. I'm counting on you to behave—get your homework done on time and keep the house clean. Laura is spending the week at the Wamplers'."

Whoa. I raised my eyebrows at Jay. This was completely unexpected. Jay's face showed no affect, but I could see the wheels turning behind his eyes. By the end of the school day on Monday, three separate people came up to me and said they'd heard my folks were out of town. And every afternoon the poolroom filled up, but nothing happened until Saturday, the day before Mom and Dad were due home.

"Molly, I'm going out with the guys tonight. I'm takin' Mom's car. What are you gonna do?"

"I'll get together with Lynn and we'll figure something out." I thought we would get Mary V.'s car, but she wasn't in a generous mood so we ended up hanging out in Lynn's room. Around 11:00

p.m., I noticed the lights go on over at my house. "Lynn, look . . . three, four, five cars over there. I bet Jay's having a party."

Curiosity and agitation mounted until we couldn't stand the suspense any longer. "C'mon, Lynn, let's go over there. I'll tell Jay I forgot my sleeping bag." We climbed the basement stairs, opened the door into the house and found about a dozen guys and girls in the den huddling, like they were planning their next play. Several of them were weaving about and slurring their words. I wondered if they had already been into Dad's liquor cabinet.

"What's going on?" we asked.

Jay turned and said, "We went to the Beacon Drive-In— you know, like we always do—about six cars of us. Jay Wright was hiding in my trunk with a cooler. Somebody brought some grain and we mixed it with beer and started drinking. Barbara Melton got completely zonked. I mean, man, she passed out cold before we got started good. The only thing we could figure out to do was bring her here. Gilmore and Crowley are back in Mom's bathroom with her now. They're trying to sober her up in the shower."

I looked at Lynn and froze. It was scary to think that some-one our age could actually pass out. The hook rug in the den had been rolled up and pushed to the side of the parquet floor. Some-one was putting an album on the stereo. The sour, putrid smell of vomit wafted down the hall.

"I guess Barbara won't be coming to mass in the morning," Lynn snickered.

Jay and a couple of the girls went down the hall to Mom's bathroom. He signaled for me to stay put. When he came back he told us that they had most of Barbara's clothes off, they were hold-ing her up under the cold shower but she wasn't coming around yet. He told them to put her in Mom and Dad's bed for a while to see if she would sleep it off.

All I could think about was how much trouble we were going to be in when Mom and Dad got home. But there was a clandes-tine, titillating feeling in the air—this seminaked person in my parents' bed.

The next morning Jay and I gathered the linens from the bed and put them in the washer and then the dryer. We didn't notice until we pulled out the white Williamsburg bedspread that Mom loved that the dryer had overheated and burned large holes in it. Jay put it on Mom's bed and rumpled it up. He may have thought he could hide the evidence and get by for a while.

But the next day when Mom and Dad returned, refreshed and rested, no mention was made of what had transpired the night before until after supper. Jay stayed in his room all afternoon sweating out a major confrontation.

When he couldn't stand it any longer, he emerged and said, "Oh . . . Mom . . . in case you are wondering . . . a few people came by last night for a few minutes and someone got sick . . . on your bed. The bedspread got a little messed up in the dryer." He bowed his head and looked at the floor as if waiting for the boom to fall.

I skipped out of the room, avoiding the Battle at Utah Beach. But as far as I could tell, nothing happened. I saw Mom and Dad talking in hushed voices but that was all. I wanted air raids and bombings, exploding hand grenades, body parts flying. Instead there was a mean kind of silence.

There would be no more drama with Jay at center stage. For Christmas that year Mom's parents gave him a trip to Europe. He left in late June. Shortly after he returned, we packed his belongings in the trunk of our car and drove him to Charlottesville, Virginia, where he entered "The University" as a first-year man. Despite his pranks, Jay could do little to dim the glow of my mother's love for him. She was lost without him and then, to make things worse, Daddy Joe died that fall.

❦

One day, in the middle of the next winter, Mom didn't get out of bed. The shades were pulled in her room and the only light came from under the bathroom door. Clothes lay in piles in the chair and on the floor. She lay curled on her side, flat like a half-deflated hot air balloon, her breathing occasionally punctuated with a moan. This shrouded form was my mother who loved light and usually switched on all the lamps the moment dusk arrived. My mother, the compulsive housekeeper, made orderly stacks and neat folds, not haphazard piles.

I paced the hall outside her room. The darkness made me fearful yet curious. I didn't understand how my mother, central command for the family, could be so sick that she stayed in bed all day.

Dad phoned Dr. Bill Grigsby, who made a house call. I thought of how many times she said, "Molly, go to your room and don't come out until you have a smile on your face." I learned to cover seething rage, indignation, and disappointment with a sweet smile. Now, all I wanted was for her to hold herself to the same standard. Why didn't she ask for me or tell me what to do? She didn't have any idea how scared I was for her, for me. Was this, somehow, my fault?

Laura came home from Thomas Jefferson Elementary School via the car pool. She was ten, six years younger than I. While Dr. Grigsby examined Mom, I reined Laura in and said, "Settle down. Mom's real sick."

Tall and prematurely gray, Dr. G. was a friend of my parents. He seemed to fill the hallway when he came out of Mom's room with his furrowed brow and tight lips. Dad followed him and we gathered in the dark paneled den which Mom had decorated with floral chintz drapes and beige linen slipcovers.

Dr. G. said, "Betsy is having a nervous breakdown. She needs a lot of rest and a peaceful environment. Girls, you help your dad now, any way you can." He rose, shook Dad's hand, and left.

Laura asked, "What's a nervous breakdown? Do I still get to go to Barbara's party at Skate Fun this Saturday?"

Dad answered Laura, "Your mother is just upset and tired. She'll be all right. And, yes, you can go." His stony tone of voice indicated the discussion was over. Laura went to our shared bedroom and changed into her jeans and sweatshirt. When she started for the door to the garage, I stopped her—"You better come home for supper in about an hour."

"Don't tell me what to do. You're not the boss of me." And off she went on her bike to the Wamplers' house.

I tiptoed back down the hall, through the den and out into the living room, making sure to close the door tightly behind me. For the last five years, I'd spent at least an hour every day practicing piano. My first inclination was to bang the hell out of those piano keys. *How dare Mom give up like this.* Instead, I opened a book of Bach inventions and stared blankly at the notes. I loved playing the piano, even scales. I was a fast learner, thanks to my instructor, Mr. O. He was exacting and easily frustrated. One day when I hadn't practiced hard enough, he threw his pencil at the floor, eraser down, and it bounced hard enough to zing upward and stick in the acoustical tiles overhead. There was another side to him that I dearly loved: he was prissy and theatrical. He once appeared at my lesson in a full-length cape with top hat and cane. I didn't need to take him into my confidence. He already surmised that things were difficult for me at home.

After a few minutes I simmered down, began to practice the C major scale as softly as I could and felt my fingers begin to sing. I forgot about Mom and Dad and played inventions until the room grew dark with the sunset.

At 10 p.m., I looked once again at the closed door and felt the weight of depression bearing down on the house, the immaculately clean house where everything had its place and stayed there for years, where you wouldn't find a sweat ring on any piece of furniture. The windows were never spotty. I thought about how Mom drew me into her compulsive cleaning ritual with a relentless drive toward perfection. "That pane is not clean enough, Molly, wash it again." Then a long, shiny pink fingernail poked me in the side. "No. Do it again."

I found Dad sitting alone in the den having a little soda with his third or fourth scotch. He was smoking and sitting up too straight on the couch with his Brooks Brothers suit still on, tie pulled loose from his neck, and collar unbuttoned. I noticed a slight quiver in Dad's voice, and he didn't look at me when he talked. He put out his cigarette in the ashtray where the butts were lined up in rows. Then he blew on his fingers two times, the way he did after every cigarette.

"When is Mom coming out of her room? How long will she be like this? Why is this happening?"

"Molly, I don't know. Your mother has been unstable for a long time. I moved the family back to Bristol because I thought it would be good for her to be near Mam and Joe." My grandparents were supportive of whatever Mom wanted to do, but they didn't appear to think much of Dad. He kicked back another swallow as if taking his own medicine.

"Is this happening because Daddy Joe died?"

"Partly. We've talked about this before. Your mother has limitations. Now you need to take over and watch after your sister. Azurine Cook from Rice Terrace is going to come during the day to fix meals and stay while you are in school." With that, he picked up his copy of *Hawaii* and started to read. This was my cue to stop asking questions. No matter how drunk he got, Dad could still turn the pages of his Book-of-the-Month Club selection. I felt sorry for him because he was disconnected, alone, and very sad, but the thought of Azurine's round, black body in the kitchen was reassuring.

Years later, Mom told me that the move to Bristol was predicated on Dad's getting the job at Mary Grey Hosiery Mills. He'd lost another ad agency job in Knoxville. Daddy Joe strong-armed his buddy, Bob Ramsey, into taking Dad on at the mill. This time he managed to hold onto the job for five years, until the company president got tired of Dad playing gin rummy and drinking with his boss.

⚘

Two weeks later, my private vigil ended when Mom opened her door and stepped into the hall. She couldn't have weighed a hundred pounds. Her slight frame seemed to cave in on itself and her hair had grown out, exposing brown roots. Ghostlike, she padded around the house barefoot wearing her white nylon gown over underwear. Her hair splayed out around her face and flattened in the back. She had dark circles around steely blue eyes. I was so happy to see her that I almost knocked her down with a hug. Immediately, she took hold of my shoulders and pushed me away.

"Let's wash this dirty hair, okay?"

I agreed and draped a towel around her shoulders. Then she leaned over the porcelain bathroom sink while I applied bright green Prell shampoo, washed and rinsed, and then set her hair. I couldn't remember the last time Mom washed my hair, but I was more than willing to do it for her. Gently, with care, I massaged her head, making sure to soap every strand of hair.

"Water too hot, Mom? Hold this cloth over your eyes to keep the soap out." She sat down in a chair so I could put curlers in her hair. I was uncertain whether she would be pleased with the end result.

"Hurry up, Molly. I'm about to pass out."

Weakness in the person who had been the backbone of the family was frightening and threw me off balance. When Mom lost it, I had to straighten up, become responsible. My internal monologue became: "Hold it in. Hold it together. Don't make waves. Keep Laura happy. Stay clear of Dad. Keep your eyes open."

❧

After a winter in hibernation, Mom decided she was feeling enough better to "come out" on Easter Sunday. Of course, she would not do that without full regalia including hat, gloves, and heels—all matching the dress that would hang from her emaciated body.

Mom was still enamored of the Jackie Kennedy look even though it had been two years since President Kennedy died. She ordered a soft, beige shift from Talbot's and planned to wear a pair of black, patent-leather shoes she already had. But the hat was a problem. She didn't have one she liked.

Though it was okay for me to drive Mom to see her therapist, it was not okay for me to drive her to town. I didn't trust her behind the wheel either, but she won the debate.

Two Saturdays before Easter Sunday, Mom said, "I need for you to go to town." She parked at the back entrance to Parks Belk department store. "Go upstairs to the women's department and bring me a couple of hats to try on. Just tell the clerk I'm in the car."

"But . . . Mo-om."

"Go on and don't waste any more time doing it."

I looked for a sales clerk in a real good mood.

"Ma'am, my mother's sick. She's in the car and can't come in. May I please take two hats out to her to try on?"

"Well, hon, we don't usually allow people to take merchandise out of the store except on approval. Just hurry back. Now which hats do you think she would like?"

I perused the whole selection and chose a black pillbox with net and grosgrain ribbon. Then I picked one with a broad brim and artificial flowers that were supposed to look like daisies. I went down the stairs and passed the hats through the window to Mom.

She adjusted the rearview mirror and set the pillbox on her head. Turning from side to side, she inspected her image while tucking a lock of hair under on one side and flipping another back on the other.

"No. This won't do. Neither will this one with the daisies. Couldn't you find something a little bit more sophisticated?"

I went back up to the third floor. "No, not these. I need two more, please." Sweat trickled down my back. Who was gonna let me have it first—Mom or this clerk?

"Okay, hon. What about this one here with the feathers?"

Again, I ran down to the car hoping Mom would be happy, hoping none of my friends would drive by and see me, hoping this would all be over soon. But it wasn't. Three more trips and the clerk was beginning to ask questions. "What's the matter with your mother anyway?" I wasn't about to tell her.

Finally, I handed over the last two hats. "Ma'am, I'm sorry but we haven't found the right one yet. Thank you." I turned and left before she had a chance to glare at me or, worse, complain.

I climbed into the passenger seat, folded my arms across my chest, faced forward and refused to say a word the whole way home. Mom was back.

☙❧

That night I lay in bed, under covers, with my jeans, sweatshirt, sneakers, pea coat, and gloves on, sweating, and waiting for Dad to turn off the lights in the den and go to bed. Then I would slip out the window and meet my best friends behind the McNeers' unoccupied house. In my mind, I was already out there. It was going to be worth it. I was going to drink some beer, real fast.

But I didn't. When I found my friends in the dark, I lost my nerve. What would happen if *I* lost control?

☙❧

On most nights, at 6:30 p.m. sharp, Mom set our plates on the table and yelled for us to take our seats. She hadn't joined us at the table since we moved across the street nearly two years before. Instead, she moved about the kitchen busying herself with the meal.

One particular night, after four or five invitations to join us, Dad stumbled in from the den where he'd been watching Walter Cronkite's evening news. It was hard to say how much he had to drink in the hour and a half since returning home from work. Bleary-eyed and disheveled, he sat down, closed his eyes, and began to eat in silence, occasionally breaking down in tears. We were accustomed to excessive moods that shifted like dunes in a windstorm.

Laura, twelve years old, ran in and took her seat, chatty about her day. She ignored Dad and left the table as soon as she could gobble down her last bite. But since I had the nonnegotiable job of drying the dishes and putting them away, I was captive. I tried to deflect their attention away from each other, shifting the winds of their disparaging remarks by asking Dad if he had his car inspected that day.

Another meal salted with tension turned to stone in my stomach. After a long pause, Dad looked up, folded his hands, and said, "You know, I might as well drive that car into a bridge abutment and get it over with."

For a moment, he had my full attention. Then I began to shut down—paralysis of the heart.

"But Dad, what about us kids? Don't we count for something?"

Before he could answer, our attention was diverted by a crash. Mom had heaved a heavy iron skillet under the cabinet to signal her disgust.

Oh God, what do I do now? Dad's falling apart and Mom is about to lose it. Then I looked at the clock. Only ten minutes until eight when Mom would disappear into her bedroom. Lights out. Door shut. TV on. *Do not fucking disturb* . . .

I looked from Mom to Dad and wished like hell I could skip out of this quicksand just as Laura had, to meet friends in the neighborhood, or talk on the phone, but tonight I was worried that Dad might follow through and self-destruct.

I followed him into the den and sat beside him on the couch, opposite the fireplace aglow with gas-burning logs. We listened to his favorite LPs: Barbra Streisand, Nancy Wilson, Henry Mancini. Dad kept drinking and talking. He told me about his work, about growing up in Mississippi, meeting William Faulkner twice, and about the death of his father when he was only thirteen. Then he talked about his service in World War II.

I knew all of the stories by heart so I just listened, hypnotized by the telling, and soaked in the details. The recitations kept Dad's mind occupied. He didn't have to think about how unhappy he was, how barren his marriage had become, how his hard work as a breadwinner was sized up by my mother's parents and found woefully lacking. I didn't want Dad to sit through another evening alone. But taking up the slack for my mother wasn't comfortable, either.

CHAPTER FOURTEEN

Digging Deeper

January 2007

Rose. I could not stop thinking about the lovely woman sitting on her daughter's sofa weeping softly as her sister recounted the tragedy of their uncle Simon's death. She appeared to be reconnecting with the loss that happened when she was a child, still experiencing the shock and grief of her parents and grandparents, the fury that could not be tamped down, the uncertainty of what would happen next—would there be justice? Later, when I got to know her better, I realized that some of those tears were for me. Rose had a deep, intuitive sense of the disappointment, shame, and dismay that I felt while coming to terms with my father's past. Because of her, Inez, and Emma, I had to do something to make things right, and at that moment all I could think to do was wrestle this story down.

❧

The NAACP was founded in New York City in 1909. By the time of the Anguilla shootings, news of the growing number of chapters around the nation and the association's success at winning court cases put fear into the hearts of my family and contributed to the hush within the white community. Maybe Dad's case was archived in the Jackson office of the NAACP. I called repeatedly and left messages but never received a call back. Meanwhile I discovered that the Library of Congress houses the NAACP files.

A researcher looked through the 1946 files but came up with nothing.

Carolyn Hackett, King Evans's daughter, told me that Elbert Hilliard, retired director of the Mississippi Department of Archives and History, might be a good source. He was in the stacks of the archives when I called. When I started to explain the nature of my research, he cut me off with, "Oh Lord, I think I know what you are talking about." My heart almost stopped. I thought he was going to tell me what really happened.

Before we could go any further, he asked about my family, where I lived, how many children I had, what kind of work I was doing. It occurred to me that this pattern of roundabout conversation was typical of the South. Indeed, it seems that exactly how southern you are is determined by your willingness to meander through a conversation.

"You see, I was nine years old when it happened. I lived in Nitta Yuma but word traveled to us. Tell me what you've found out already."

I went through the long list of people I had talked with and research I had done. I figured an archivist to be a lover of history, and I expected him to open up. He told me that he just couldn't comment on the shootings in '46 because he and his wife attend the same church that Aunt Lib does. He explained that he thought a lot of my gracious aunt and wouldn't want to diminish his standing in her eyes. Besides, I'd already told him more than he knew. His comments didn't satisfy me. A historian—a man who spent his working life and now his volunteer hours helping people re-create their past—wouldn't help me. His propriety, silence, and social connections trumped his professional ethics so his mind was closed to fairness, and I was discovering that to be true for many of his generation. Later I learned that Mr. Hilliard spent his career years walking through political minefields to get funding for his agency. That might explain his conservatism.

Penny Weaver at the Southern Poverty Law Center returned my call and told me that there was no information available in their files. The center is examining cases that go back to the 1960s.

She could not help me. I asked her about the potential for legal issues to arise as a result of my investigation. Dad's cousin had warned me that civil rights workers were still in Mississippi prisons and I could be in danger. Again, it seemed that anyone left alive from that time would probably still be living in the world of bigotry, silence, and fear. Penny scoffed and told me that those fears were totally unfounded. I remembered that the bus boycott in Montgomery didn't occur until 1955. The following year, in September, the Klan rallied in Montgomery. Dr. King had urged, "Let me ask you to be sane and rational." He called for dignity and reasonableness. I wonder how my father reacted to the Alabama events that came a decade later.

☙

Early afternoon, in June of 1975, in Atlanta, Georgia, my doorbell rang. I remember this moment as clearly as if it were last year instead of decades ago. My mother stood outside the screen door looking frayed. Bright sunshine was behind her, so I didn't see the dark circles that shadowed her darting eyes until she entered the apartment. Her shoulders slumped forward. She wore beige linen pants and a matching sweater, and her hair was frosted and teased, but her carefully applied makeup didn't completely hide her agitation. She clasped her car keys in both hands as if to make sure she didn't lose the one thing that brought her to safety.

I encouraged Mom to come in and asked what in the world was going on that she would show up without calling ahead. She was supposed to be at home in Virginia with Dad.

She stepped onto the sculpted gold carpet, mashed flat by twenty-five years of coming and going in the apartment my husband and I now shared as its new residents. He was down at Five Points, Atlanta's financial and legal hub, becoming a big-city lawyer.

Mom headed for the sofa, sat down, and covered her eyes to keep me from seeing her cry. She was as vulnerable as if she were standing naked in the middle of a crowd. My instinct was to gather her in, but I was careful not to sit too close to her. Over the course of the next two hours, I learned that my parents were splitting up. Then Mom settled back into the cushions, depleted. I tried not to show any emotion except sympathy while I listened hard and occasionally reached over to pat her knee. I told her it was okay that she had come to me, but as I said this, my heart went into revolt. *No, no, no. Go back to Dad. I can't take care of you.*

I asked her what had happened. "I'm not surprised really, but after almost thirty years, what made you finally do it?"

"I can't live another day under the same roof with him."

Sitting beside Mom on the wheat-colored Danish-modern sofa that we had purchased with one of the first paychecks, the intimacy felt too new, too fragile. *It won't be long until she's in charge again.*

In my mind I tabulated all of the possible reasons for her leaving Dad. I was not aware of anything dramatic that had changed in their life together. Dad's drinking had been a problem for a very long time. He'd struggled to launch his own advertising agency with Mom's financial help. I knew she resented throwing her money down a bottomless well.

She said, "He stays drunk. I believe he starts at the office, maybe before lunch. He's bankrupt, and he's mad because I won't give him any more money. I can't." The reality began to take shape in my mind when I thought about my brother and me, both married, and Laura out of the house at the University of Tennessee. My husband and I had given Mom her first grandchild just five months ago. Knowing her as I did, I realized that there was a confluence of forces at work to wrench her from an intolerable marriage. She had an empty nest, she was beginning to recognize the onset of "old age," and her chance to accomplish something long dreamed of had finally arrived.

Then, she took a deep breath and squared her shoulders, as if a dark cloud had just passed beyond the sun. "I still have the Fleming building in Florida. It's the last one. I can live off of that." Her eyes brightened; her shoulders relaxed.

I asked her where Dad was.

"At home. I left him in the house. All I have with me is a trunk-load of clothes." Her forest-green Mercedes was parked by the curb. Purchased after my grandmother's estate sale, the car was tangible evidence that Mom was ready to take care of herself, to have something she wanted, to own her life. But getting a divorce was still an earth-shaking decision with consequences way out in front of her. None of her friends were divorced. She always considered it "common" and beneath her as women of her era did, especially in the South.

"Does Dad believe you?"

"He knows I'm serious. I talked to a lawyer yesterday, then called to tell him to get out. I don't want to be home when he packs to move."

I didn't say anything for several minutes, giving her time. Into the stillness came the sound of a baby girl, stirring and waking from her nap. Mom stood up, smoothed her pants, shaped her hair, and wiped mascara from under her eyes as if Whitney could tell she'd been crying. We walked down the hall to the nursery and lifted my warm, stretching baby into her arms. The sweetness and innocence in my child's sleepy eyes brought Mom and me together in a shared smile and the soft glow of hope.

❦

Mom stayed on at the apartment for two days, sleeping on the couch and vacillating between euphoric relief and utter devastation. My husband was cordial and patient with Mom but left even earlier for work and came home after seven at night.

On the morning she left us, we hugged on the front porch in the sunshine. "Are you sure you're ready to take on this battle, Mom?"

"It has to happen. I can't take him back now. But listen, Molly, I don't have the strength to call your brother and sister. Please do that for me."

I nodded yes, while my heart said *NO.*

ᐧᑫᐧ

After a month I decided that I needed to go to Bristol to visit my dad. He had moved into a furnished chalet on the side of a hill, the "treehouse," as he called it. Mom was safely resettled in the house on Long Crescent Drive.

On the surface, Dad was delighted to see me and to have his granddaughter in his new digs. We made a cradle for her in the bottom drawer of the dresser. She was sweet, slept for long stretches, and when awake, cooed and smiled and studied his face. But, deep down, he was lost, completely lost. My mother's financial support finally severed, Dad felt deeply insecure. The friends they shared over the years had left him in the cold. It seemed he had reached the nadir of his life.

Meanwhile, Mom was beginning to rebound. She made plans to sell the house and move across town. When I went by to check on her, she told me that she woke up every morning with a smile on her face. I could tell just by her outward appearance that she would be all right, even better than before.

But she wasn't happy that I had been so solicitous and concerned about my father. While I was visiting her, she took me aside and divulged more gruesome details of their life together. I sat patiently through her rant but when she started divulging details too personal for a daughter's ears, I tensed and had a strong desire to get up and leave for home.

After we returned to Atlanta, Dad wrote my daughter, Whitney, the following letter:

How wonderful it was to have you and your beloved mother visit in Granddad's house! My heart ached to see you off at the airport. My squirrels, my birds, my trees are sad today because you are gone—but, like me, they know you will return and all of us can hardly wait.

Your Granddad will treasure all his life your look of recognition when he came for you yesterday. You did

recognize me, and grin, and I am thrilled to have gained
that at your very young age.

Molly, you will never know how much your visit home
meant to your family at this desolate time. I particularly
needed your love and understanding and friendship. As
always, I received it in full measure.

With all my love,
Dad and Granddad

1977 was a big year. Whitney was two when my husband decided
he needed to move back to Bristol so he could keep an eye on his
family's business and practice law. I didn't want to leave Atlanta.
Big city life thrilled me. I felt less burdened because of the degree
of privacy and anonymity I had there. Life was sweet and good.

We moved anyway, in April, and to my surprise, Mom and Dad
were both in new relationships and both planning to get married
again. Mom, at fifty years old, had fallen in love with a bachelor
the same age. Will was infinitely sociable and fun. They slipped off
with friends and didn't invite me or my siblings to their wedding.
For the next nine years, while Will remained cancer free, they ran
a travel agency and skipped around the world. It was the happiest
time of my mother's life.

Dad and Julia were married in the church and held their recep-
tion at my house. Julia was lovely but intense. She buoyed my
father's ego by singing his praises openly and often. They honey-
mooned in Greece and started their new life together. With both
my parents settled in loving relationships, my involvement with
them eased. I was able to focus on my daughter, who was soon
fighting for attention with another baby girl. Until Kate was one
and a half, I stayed home and watched them develop into hearty
little girls—very unlike each other in temperament and personality.
Then I worked part-time and prepared for a new role as teacher.

February 14, 2008

Looking out my study window into the naked forest with the
chaos and destructive side of nature so apparent, fallen tree

trunks, strainers along the bank of the river, occasional sleet and ice, I decided I needed time away from the computer. A drive back to the Delta might lead to some new discoveries. I organized my lists so as to be efficient with the four days I had free in my teaching schedule. The first day out I drove the ten boring and laborious hours to Jackson, Mississippi. The next morning I set out for the Mississippi Department of Archives and History, but first I made several phone calls. In each case the voice on the other end sounded unenthusiastic except for Inez, Simon's niece. She had had surgery and wasn't able to meet me in Anguilla, but I was invited to her home in Greenville.

I tried to find Elbert Hilliard at the archives. He would have a difficult time hedging my questions if I met him in person. He was out of town. I worked with several reference librarians and checked the Sovereignty Commission reports online. There was no mention of Dad. Then I went through the *Jackson Advocate* and several other black newspapers. I found no reference to the shootings but read a number of editorials admonishing blacks to take responsibility for their lives. There were write-ups of lynchings and other heinous acts in other southern states, but little about what was happening racially in Mississippi. I guessed that Dad's incident was too close to home, and coverage might have created negative backlash.

Earlier in the month I had signed up for the nine-weeks-long Building Bridges course in Asheville. The small-group format encouraged dialogue between the races, and synchronously, I met a white civil rights worker who had spent time in Mississippi in the '60s. It became clear to me right away that the gaunt, grey-haired, intense man had been a dedicated activist all of his life. After a discussion one evening, Charlie Thomas took me aside. He had listened intently to my story about Dad. When I told him I was preparing to drive back to the Delta to look for physical evidence of what happened, he said, "You'll only find information in oral history from living adults who can still recollect the time." I had grown to respect his perspective because of the struggles he had witnessed firsthand. When I came up empty-handed at the archives, I left for Rolling Fork in search of voices.

The drive deep into the Delta presented a very different land-scape—fallow fields with just a hint of cotton on brown stalks, bare trees with clumps of mistletoe hanging in the branches. It was rainy and quiet on the highway. The sky was wide and there were thousands of birds flying in lines like strings on the tails of kites.

From the courthouse I made several calls. Robert Morgen-field, brother of Muddy Waters, famous blues musician from Rolling Fork, would not have time to see me. He had an all-day business meeting at his church. I called two older black ladies. One of them hung up on me. The other one said, "I don't know nothin' 'bout your people."

I stopped by to visit with Mrs. Evans, only to find that her daughter had asked a relative to be present during my visit. The distrust, the closed mouths, the shutting doors left me feeling defeated and unwanted, like a pariah—to be avoided at all cost.

As I drove toward Greenville to visit with Inez, two thoughts came to me. First, black people are used to remaining sequestered and keeping their information to themselves and each other. Second, I imagined them saying, "Why should I talk to this white woman about her family? Why should I share information with a white person?" Perhaps the time had come for me to kick the deep southern dust off my feet and head for home.

⚜

Inez met me at the door in a leopard skin caftan and black slip-pers trimmed in black fur. Her house was lovely, immaculate, rather ornately decorated, warm and cozy. There were candles everywhere, some burning. We sat on a camel-colored leather couch in her den. The TV was on but not so loud that we couldn't hear each other talk. Presidential candidate Obama was speaking. Inez expressed her delight in him.

She looked weak and tired. Her doctor had stripped veins from both legs. She talked to me about her daughter's family and the fact that her son was in jail. When I told her that people in Anguilla were hushed up again, she said, "You know, there is something, somebody keeping a secret that you need to know but you may not get to know."

And then she said this: "You are marching to a different drummer. Do you know that? You are doing it for a bigger reason. Pray. And ask God to show the way and pray that God opens the minds and hearts of people like your aunt so that they will open up to you." She wondered how people like Dad or Bill could live their whole lives with the death of two innocent people on their hands and not become insane. She told me that she didn't think it fair that Dad had to live with the burden of guilt all his life if he didn't do it.

Those words, the kindness of Inez, the warm embrace as we parted, lifted me out of despair and into hope. If no other person could understand the paradoxes in my own heart, Inez could, and I felt peace because of her.

I called Jay from the road to tell him about my trip. Disillusion and frustration in my voice must have registered with him. Both of us had attended Al-Anon meetings for years, hoping to learn life skills that would replace stale, useless coping strategies we learned living with Dad. We spoke the same language. When I got home I had an e-mail from him:

> When you're out there, and there is nobody else around you except the breath of your higher power, which comes in as wind in your face, you are pressing against the sides of the known world. I think that's what Inez means. In that remote land, it takes two to tango. You and God. The dance, however, is great stuff. I think Dad had a huge emotional capacity and I think the shooting was a private burden, even though Bill very well may have shot the boys. Personally, I don't think the idea of "carrying guilt" would have weighed in much if he didn't actually shoot anyone; it's likely, however, he would have felt the guilt of being part of it. Tom may have too. But I know Tom well enough to know that he let all of that fall into the world of forgiveness. Tom understood the essence of the

twelve steps, for sure. If Dad had gone there, I think it would have "cracked open the melon" so to speak.

The great green heron that had wintered on my little stretch of riverbank still stalked the water's edges for small fish. Canada geese used the flyway as a guide to northern destinations. The mallards swam up and down and mated. One mother cruised with her nine babies—it was thrilling to watch the little ones skitter across rocks and skim across the surface to keep up with her. I saw otters, muskrats, wild turkeys, a coyote. The stark trunks of trees that angled over the water filled out with green. I put up a hammock and a rope swing and one day drove upriver a mile with a friend, and we put our tubes in the cool water after the heat settled in. It took over three hours to wind our way back down to the house. The gentle lazy flow of the river induced contented living, but I was still perplexed and obsessive about the family story. I wrote, I contemplated, and I made more phone calls.

At last a hefty file of papers arrived from a title searcher in Jackson. She sent a schedule of all land transactions into and out of my great-grandfather's and Thomas's estates, the records of which she had combed to find a deed for acreage in Sharkey County conveyed to Simon Toombs. Included in the packet were my grandfather's will, a list of assets including such things as mules, planters, cultivators, tractors, mowing machines, a deed of trust set forth and conveying allowances to Dad and his siblings, a support payment to Mamaw in the sum of four thousand dollars for the first year after Thomas died. Nothing was legally deeded directly from my grandfather to Simon, as I'd heard might be the case.

I called my lawyer, and she assured me that, deed or no deed, the issue of land could not be contested now. That was beside the point for me—I wanted to know if Simon and I were part of the same family.

CHAPTER FIFTEEN

Sis

February 2008

After months of being stymied, I sat with the unresolved story until I felt a nudge to revisit a primary source, Aunt Sis. Maybe time had softened her resolve to keep the secret to herself. I wrote her a letter setting out my findings and asked if she would talk with me again. On Sunday, February 20, she called after writing out her response to my letter.

She started the conversation by giving me some context for the time in which the shootings occurred.

"You have to remember that Tom and Jay were barely home from World War II and they had trained hard and served in the war. Your daddy was only twenty-four, and Tom was twenty-two. If you do your research, you'll find that the NAACP was all over Mississippi and they had lawyers ensconced in the state capitol in Jackson. Whatever versions you have acquired from Tommy and Lib are secondhand hearsay as far as I'm concerned. Likewise anything told you by the descendents of the victims. Everyone involved is deceased save your mother and me."

Sis did not know that two men were shot, she didn't know that the incident had been in the newspapers, and she was told, by Bill, not to discuss it with anyone.

"Okay. What I know to be true is that I was in transit by train from Columbia, Missouri, to Memphis at the time of the incident. I left by train for Leland as my mother could not come for me in Memphis as had been planned. In Leland, I was met by Bill. I, of course, knew something was wrong. For the next hour Bill told me what had happened—in detail—and cautioned me about the fact that the NAACP was all around and that that was causing a lot of concern and it was best to keep it to ourselves and not discuss it. When I got home, Mother was in her bed with a black handkerchief over her head and Tom was in the boys' room sitting up in bed. I don't remember any discussion of what had happened over the *joyful* Christmas holiday." The word "joyful," spoken with gutteral emphasis, was not the only word used in sarcasm.

"I do remember spending a lot of time with Betsy next door visiting with my nephew. I went to all of the Christmas parties and dances and tried to stay removed from the scene, as it were. Not one friend or social acquaintance ever broached the subject with me. Then or ever. And in that time everyone respected personal privacy among their families and friends. They did not gossip about each other's bad times. We lived in a very closed and protected society in which we were very, very much the minority. I do not know where you are trying to go with all of this mystery as you call it, but I would caution you not to pursue this. Your search for blame may well lie in your own guilt in regard to your father.

"Bill has four daughters who live in Mississippi and our family owns the family land and the gin property in Anguilla. I don't think it is appropriate or admirable to put their well-being and sensitivities in jeopardy by your desire to shed light on this darkness, as you put it, in our family's past. I'd just let it go, Molly. I think you are barking up the family tree. I would pray that out of respect for me and your own children and all of us who are proud to be roots and branches of the Fields tree, you will leave us at peace even if you can't find peace in yourself.

"I don't know what your mother told you but she was the only one there but she wasn't an eyewitness so everybody else is gone. She was a young woman of twenty-four, a young woman in a strange land and probably hysterical. She was there, I wasn't. Judging from my seventy years' experience of Miss Fields and her boys, I'm pretty sure what happened. I am almost positive that Bill was not on the site at the time the trigger was pulled but he did come upon the results of the actions immediately thereafter.

He had been given another chore so was late getting there." I did not argue Bill's role. To do so might have enflamed Sis and caused her to shut down.

"As for the Pan Am station, there were many knifings, killings, stabbings, and drunkenness with the black population there— many of whom were our own employees. They were often beaten up and taken to the hospital in Vicksburg by our family. It was a constant source of concern in our community and those who cared about their black employees and their families. The boys were brave in their intentions but they were very foolish to go into such a place.

"If you really want to get into the guilt part of it, and I could get into it with you and I could tell you where the guilt lies but I don't really want to do that because I don't want to disillusion you about anyone else. I have tried on my own to write the family history for my kids and I had to stop in the middle of it because of that. Because I don't want to change their minds and their feelings about people in the family. The real instigator of it and pursuer of it had nothing to do with your father. Or Tom or Bill, okay? The boys were misguided and urged to go to a scene where they had no business going, but once they put themselves there, they were in great danger." Sweat broke out on my forehead and began to trickle down my temples. She was a tiny flicker away from a bonfire—any disagreement—she'd have thrown me in it.

"You've written all of this down—to what end?"

"I have no idea why I've been captivated by the incident except that it is a story that has ramifications for lots of people. It potentially has the ability to create some reconciliation, some forgiveness and understanding."

"Reconciliation and forgiveness for whom, for what?"

⚭

The longer we talked, the nastier the conversation became. Sis heard my own resolve and determination. When I could not be dissuaded from continuing my investigation, she became accusatory and tried to shame me into silence.

"It happened. I do understand what happened and I do understand why it happened. There are all sorts of extenuating circumstances here and for all practical purposes let me tell you that it was pretty much in self-defense. You'll just have to go along with that. As I said, people just didn't talk about these things. Even if you lived in that place at that time you would understand that. Families took care of their own business and respected each other and so far as telling anybody, I don't know anybody that knows anything about it and Lib knows practically nothing. She's the only one that has kids up there and they own everything that's left. They do business there. It's not a safe place as you know too because of the horrible poverty. That's another place I can't stand to go because it's so depressing and there doesn't seem to be any way to get out of it. At that time in the 1940s, everyone was coming out of World War II in shock and families had lost people and one thing and another. It was a tough time." Extenuating circumstances? I wanted to kick myself for not having the backbone to ask that question.

"I know my brothers well enough to know that in the many, many conversations that we had that went on for hours and hours, on my front porch about all the sadness that was in our lives growing up as kids and there was a lot of it, this was an issue that happened and it was bad and not good and there wasn't anything we could do about it. Basically, you need to put things in proper perspective. If you want to start stirring the stink up, and this letter you wrote me—I couldn't believe it. It's ridiculous. You're the one that's doing it. Give that some thought. You have two daughters, don't you want to protect them?"

☙

I hung up the phone and paced the house to calm myself.

It was clear to me that she believed Bill's story—that Dad and Tom went to the Pan Am that night with some ulterior motive—perhaps encouraged by someone else. But who?

Mamaw might have instructed Bill to tell Sis as little as possible but to exclude him from the scene would have been an outright lie. And if it was, he may have lied about his complicity too. I struggled, hard, with the notion of family honor, as I had done for many months. It all boiled down to honor versus truth. I reasoned that this far out on the limbs of the family tree, it was important that truth reign, if possible.

But why did Sis feel a need to assign guilt to me? I could only think that it had to do with one phone conversation that I had with her. When I was in college, Mamaw and Sis drove to Bristol together to confront Dad about his drinking. Today it would be called an intervention, but ultimately it didn't work. They demanded that Dad check himself into a rehab hospital in Asheville so that he could dry out and get some therapy. On my next visit home, I asked, "Dad, how was your time at Appalachian Hall?"

"Well . . . it was a worthless expense of time and money. I didn't see a psychiatrist the whole time I was there. Since nobody was talking to me, I slipped out to my car where I had a fifth in the glove compartment and had a toot whenever I wanted one."

Several years after this, Mom and Dad were living apart; I was married and had two children. Dad was alone and probably binging. Sis called my house one night when I was preparing a meal for company. "You need to do something about your dad. Don't you care? Look at it this way. Alcoholism is a disease just like diabetes. You need to put your father in the hospital before his drinking kills him." She did not appreciate my refusal to get involved. Too much energy had already been expended. I knew I didn't have the power to turn a rock into a tree. I couldn't elicit the help of my siblings. Laura had three children and worked full time. She had no reserve energy to take on our father. Jay didn't have the will or the desire to go up against Dad.

❧

Soon after the phone call from Sis, during the '90s, my lap was full of critical concerns, ones that eclipsed the problem of Dad's drinking. His wife, Julia, died of stomach cancer. One afternoon she asked Dad to call for me, to come sit by her bed. I made a pot of cold potato soup and took it to her. She couldn't sip it because her lips and mouth were so badly ulcerated from radiation and chemo. She lay with her eyes closed, occasionally opening them to make sure I was still there. Periodically, her breathing stopped. Each time I thought that she was gone, but a belated gasp erupted at the last second. The right words—any words at all—would not come to me. I felt inept and doltish in the face of death. Dad took Julia to the hospital after he returned home from the office. That night, she drifted off in a morphine haze and died.

Two years later my mother's husband, Will, died after battling cancer for twelve years. I was with my mother when she decided to let him go. The doctor removed the breathing tube. He faded away. My heart broke for her and for the man who had become fatherlike to me.

In between these two losses, my husband was diagnosed with a tumor in his sphenoid sinus. The ENT doctor tried to biopsy it in the clinic at the University of Virginia hospital. His instrument slipped and severed the carotid artery nearby. For three days the doctors worked to repair the damage. They kept finding me in the neurological intensive care waiting room and saying, "If he makes it through the next twenty-four hours . . ." Five surgeries later, I took him home for a long, slow recuperation, grateful that he had survived.

After these losses and near losses, I had to face the stark reality that my bookstore, which had been in operation from 1991 to 1996, was not going to continue as a viable business. Though it was hard work with long hours, I had painstakingly created an atmosphere that was open, friendly, stocked with fabulous books, and frequently the site of community gatherings with regular signings by prominent regional authors. Book Ends became a giant sandbox for me and my girls. I had been an avid reader all my life and loved the feel of a good book in my hands. But Books-A-Million and Super Walmart moved into our town of forty-five thousand, and they were selling books for the wholesale price that

I paid for them. I withstood the decline in sales as long as I could and then shut the door. In the midst of all this loss, I realized that another one was headed my way. Though I had had the audacity to think that my own marriage would not end in divorce—I was wrong. In 1998, our long relationship began to unravel. Not long before the final decree, Dad died.

CHAPTER SIXTEEN

Dad's Final Days

Mid-August 2000, Uncle Tom called to tell me that Dad was in the De Funiak Springs hospital in Florida.

"What's wrong?" I asked—as if I didn't already know that too much alcohol for too many years was high on the list.

"He has congestive heart failure and a massive aortic aneurism. I had a real hard time getting him to go to the hospital because he didn't want to give up his cigarettes. Finally, when we got there, I asked Dr. Stewart to put a nicotine patch on him and give him whatever it would take to keep him from having the d.t.'s. Things have settled down now. But you might want to come down here and see about him."

I hung up and called Jay immediately. We decided to meet in Charlotte and fly down. I prepared for the trip with tug-of-war emotions. Yes, I wanted to see my dad again. No, I didn't.

Before noon the following day, Jay and I arrived at Uncle Tom's apartment, right next door to Dad's. He was happy to see us. Tom was thin as a post, swarthy from working in the sun on a golf course for years, and full of dry, down-to-earth humor. "By all rights your Dad ought to be dead already. He's been drinkin' so long his insides are pickled."

❦

I was first to enter the sterile, stark-white and pale-green hospital room. Dad was sitting up in bed when I knocked and then poked my head around the bed screen.

"Hello, Parge," he said. That was one of several nicknames he had for me, including Mol, Pol, and Pod Wadis. "I didn't know you were coming . . . Jay, how are you, son?"

The first thing I noticed about him was his sallow skin, the bulging and bloodshot eyes framed in long black lashes; this was a different man from the one I'd seen in a photo taken six months earlier. He was standing on the deck of Aunt Sis's house with Uncle Bill, Uncle Tom, and Aunt Sis. He looked dapper in his double-breasted navy blazer, the pinstripe Brooks Brothers shirt that I sent him for Christmas that year, and a rep tie. He was sunburned and robust and I could tell that being enfolded in his family suited him well after years of isolation and poverty in Bristol.

"Dad, you feelin' bad?" I asked.

"No, not really. I went to the VA hospital in Pensacola for a checkup and the doctor put me in here. I'll be going home soon. Gosh, it's good to see you kids." He lifted himself up, sliding his legs over the side of the bed. I blushed when his loosely tied hospital gown rode up.

Tom spoke. "Well, young Jay, s'pose we go over to the club and hit a round of golf. We can come back later and pick up Molly for some supper at Gino's."

"Sounds good to me."

Why didn't I anticipate this? Of course Jay was going to go off in the only car we had with Uncle Tom and leave me here, alone with Dad.

"Molly, do you want us to drop you off at the inn?"

Surprise, surprise. It took me a minute to consider my options. I knew that it would be hard to stay, but this might be my only chance to be with Dad alone.

"You go ahead. I'll stay here."

After Jay and Tom left I tried unsuccessfully to engage Dad in conversation. I ran through my list: my girls, my teaching, my divorce.

We went on like this for half an hour when his one-word answers became grunts and nods. I could see that he was agitated and I wondered about d.t.'s. Then he asked me, "Molly, could you get me a cigarette?"

"Dad, you're in the hospital. They won't let you smoke in here." He lay back and became quiet. It was clear he was struggling and the tension in the room began to mount. I felt so awkward. *What do I talk about with this man who is my father but seems like a stranger?* I wish I had known, then, about the Anguilla shoot-out. I could have asked my father, the very person accused of killing two black men, what really happened that night. Would I have had the courage to ask? Yes. Would he have talked to me—openly and honestly? I believe he would have. Chewed up and spit out by life, he must have known that death had him in its sights.

"Molly, are you sure I can't have just one cigarette?"

"I'm sure, Dad. This is a nonsmoking facility. I don't have a car to go and get them for you and I wouldn't even if I could. You're pretty sick, Dad, or you wouldn't be here."

My refusal brought our communication to a halt. The silence brought on by the things we could not talk about took on form and substance and began to crawl up and cover the walls like kudzu. I sat back in my chair, put my feet up on the bed rail, and looked down at the book of crossword puzzles I had picked up at the airport. But instead of filling them in, I started to frame a dialogue in my head. And I simmered, then boiled. *Dad, I needed for you to be a father, a kind and good, safe, and respectable man.* I looked over at Dad where he lay back, eyes closed. *Thank God. He can't hear my thoughts . . . For God's sake, Molly, he's dying.* I wiped the sweat off my forehead and noticed how hard I was breathing. I stood up, walked out of the room and down the hall to the water fountain, took a drink, and kept walking until I was outside the hospital. The sun was so hot, it had to be over a hundred, and I was already cooking on the inside. I walked back to Dad's room, sat back down, and watched his chest rise and fall.

Late in the afternoon, Dad woke up. It was a good thing. I'd been fighting Armageddon in my head. I was exhausted. The kudzu shrank back down the walls and disappeared. The nurse came in to check Dad's vitals and when his supper came at 4:00, I felt myself deflate, let go, and relax.

As if he had a sixth sense and knew the coast was clear, Dad rallied and looked over at me. For the next half hour, we talked casually about inane topics. Didn't matter what was said, there was an ease and comfort that transcended words. I studied Dad's face and then his body. The distended belly, the shaking hands, the feet so swollen with edema that they were rock hard, the toenails untended for God knows how long. I felt a softness coming into my heart and an ache, no, a stabbing pain of sadness for having become so inured to such a diseased and wounded man.

At supper, Tom talked about how happy Dad had been since arriving in Florida three years before. "Oh, he didn't slow down on his drinking but somehow he managed to get and keep a job reporting for the *De Funiak Herald*. He loved to go down to the air force base at Fort Walton to report on activities down there. He had a way of getting a good story out of people."

Jay and I went back to the inn that night and sat outside with a couple of beers. We talked about Dad in soft voices. We knew that he wouldn't be around long.

Uncle Tom called to wake me up and say he'd come over to the hospital after church. While I was in the shower washing my hair, I thought about the day before. It occurred to me that the time I spent with Dad was perfect. I asked for help and it came in an unexpected way. It came in the form of peace. Dad and I were in the same room together for almost three hours. It was hard, at first, but later it was easy—as easy as it had ever been. On a subterranean level, I knew that it was too late to have a substantive conversation with Dad.

I rallied Jay and we decided to go to the historic De Funiak Inn for a full breakfast before we left for the hospital.

"Dad might die while we're on the way home, but I feel really good about coming down here. It was good for me to be stuck at the hospital yesterday afternoon. A big part of me wants to cut and run whenever I'm around Dad. I had no choice but to sit there."

"I couldn't wait to get out of there. Sorry I left you but Uncle Tom has been more of a father to me than Dad ever was."

"I know, Jay, sometimes he seems so out of touch with reality. I guess it's the alcohol."

We spent the afternoon in Dad's room reminiscing and talking politics. Jay took a break, changed into shorts, and went for a run. While he was out, I turned to Dad.

"Would you like me to rub some of this lotion on your back, Dad?"

"That'd be okay."

I took the free bottle of lotion from Dad's bedside table and began to work some moisture into the dry skin of his back. He sat very still and quiet. Occasionally, he said, "That feels good, Polly." After that, I walked around the bed, knelt in front of him and worked the lotion into his calves and reluctantly onto the taut skin of his feet. As I worked, I noticed Dad letting go and softening. I looked up into his eyes, his tired and distant eyes, and saw that they were wet. This poor man. He had not been touched or loved in a lifetime. It broke my heart wide open.

After Jay returned and washed off the sweat in the bathroom sink, we gave Dad a hug and told him good-bye. Just before I left him, I turned and said, "I love you, Dad."

He echoed back, "I love you, too." And I knew he meant it.

ॐ

Jay and I were back in our respective homes for four days when Uncle Tom called from Florida. He said, "Your dad is in a coma. I asked Dr. Stewart to have him transferred to the Crestview Hospital. And I asked the Episcopal priest to give him last rites or whatever they do in these matters. You better get down here right away if you want to see him again."

The next day we drove into Fort Walton during a formidable thunderstorm. The sky was pitch black. Low-hanging clouds pelted the rental car with sheets of rain. Every few minutes the darkness gave way to a flash of lightning and an angry retort of thunder. Driving became tedious and slow which made me even more anxious to get there. The fact that Dad was in a coma did not lessen my desire to see him and, yes, even talk to him. I had a sense that he would still be able to hear me even if "the shades were pulled and the lights were out."

Jay and I sprinted across the parking lot to the hospital lobby and the receptionist's desk. I asked, "Can you give me a room number for H. J. Fields?" She explained that the power had just returned and her computer was booting up again.

I wanted to say to her, "Step on it, lady. Our father might die while you wait around. Don't you have a list somewhere?"

When she was able, she typed in Dad's name and looked up, "We don't have a patient by that name." Glitch. He had to be there. *Uncle Tom wouldn't have moved him again.* Maybe the computer accidentally deleted Dad's name? Then it dawned on me.

Jay and I looked into each other's eyes and knew that Dad was gone. We hadn't made it in time for our last good-byes. For a change, my tears didn't hesitate; they came in a flash. We were directed to the third floor where a nurse met us at the elevator and took us to Dad's room. At first, I didn't want to go in. Maybe it would be better not to carry an image of his dead body in my memory. The shock of losing a parent registered on my personal Richter scale.

Somehow, I convinced myself to go into his room. Stretched out on the bed, covered by a sheet, was my father. I peeled back the cover to see that his chest was still. At first, I felt like Sleepy peering at the glass case where Snow White's body lay. But there was no beating heart, no hope of animation. At that moment, I looked up to the ceiling and all around the room. *Where are you, Dad?* Just in case he was watching me from some ethereal place, I bent over and kissed the cold cheek. For half a second I thought about shaking him to see if he would come back.

I wanted him to know that I tried . . . I tried to get to him before he died. I wanted him to know that despite the challenges of our relationship I still loved him in the end. Such a conflicted parent, capable of goodness, capable of destruction.

I backed out of his room and found Jay in the hall shifting rest-lessly from one foot to the other. "What do we do now?"

Then I made a decision that reflected a gross lack of sanity. "Jay, we're here; we have arrangements to make; let's stay the weekend and clean out Dad's apartment before we go back home."

"I'll need to make some phone calls for work but I guess you're right. I don't want to have to come back down here in a few weeks."

"Why don't you stay with Uncle Tom in his extra bedroom? I'll stay at Dad's."

"Are you sure you want to stay in Dad's apartment?"

"I'll be all right." This was one of those times when my head said yes while my heart threw itself on the floor. All I really knew was that I was exhausted. I didn't want to share a room with any-one else, stay at Uncle Tom's, or even spend the night in a hotel room by myself.

We got to Dad's apartment around 7:00 p.m. It was still light outside and I could open the curtains and see the job ahead. Only one bulb still lit in an overhead fixture. The place was a disaster. The living room had an old couch and a couple of side chairs which belonged to my grandmother. A card table was set up in the corner, covered in stacks of papers. Strewn on the carpet were half-finished *New York Times* crossword puzzles, library books, and crumbs. There was a worn, food-stained path from the galley kitchen to Dad's favorite reading chair. I wrote my name in the dust on the coffee table and walked into the kitchen which had a sink full of dishes that were dirtied weeks ago. The fridge reeked. I found a George Foreman grill on the countertop that had layers of grease—probably going back to the first time Dad used it. I walked down the hallway past the bathroom, pausing to see if it was clean enough for me to use. The linoleum floor was stained, the shower curtain black with mildew. Half-empty bottles of aftershave lined the shelves of the medicine cabinet along with umpteen prescriptions. There *was* toilet paper—thanks, Dad.

Farther down the hall were two bedrooms, one empty except for boxes of prints and old photos from Dad's apartment in

Bristol—empty suitcases, an old Olivetti typewriter, and a closet full of winter clothes.

In his bedroom, next door, was an unmade bed with one pillow, sheets with cigarette burns, and no covers. There was a dresser full of clothes, some brand new from L. L. Bean. On the dresser top were coins, combs, and a picture of his beloved Julia.

I started a grocery list including extra-large leaf bags, cleaning supplies, bottled water. I found myself standing in the middle of the living room, sad, overwhelmed, and sickened by the trappings of a diseased life.

ᘒᘖ

Jay and Uncle Tom were outside in the white plastic chairs on the second-floor deck that the apartment shared with two others. Tom smoked cigars and talked about how he needed to quit before his emphysema killed him, too. I took a seat and shook my head.

"I guess you noticed that your dad didn't own a vacuum," Uncle Tom said with a snicker.

A train whistled in the distance and chugged in our direction. There was a small garden in the backyard bordered by a stand of bamboo. Just beyond that was the train track.

For the next hour we watched dusk disappear into darkness. Jay and I listened to Tom drone on about the neighbors and how everybody looked out for Dad and had patience with his drinking. When he moved to the subject of Woodberry Forest, Tom's and Jay's alma mater, I knew it was time for me to turn in.

I was careful not to let my toothbrush make contact with any surface in Dad's bathroom. I pulled on a tee shirt and a pair of shorty pajama bottoms. It was hard to see anything, but I foraged around, located top and bottom sheets that appeared to be clean, and put them on the bed. I thought about how Dad would never come back to this place again. And I started to feel creeped out.

Geez, I've gotta be nuts. Maybe I just won't sleep. The atmosphere in the apartment was laden with a thick aroma of stale cigarette smoke. I located a half-empty pack on the table beside Dad's chair. I took it to the empty bedroom, raised the window, lit up and blew the smoke out the screen as if to preserve a more pristine environment than the one I was in. In the previous ten years, I'd bummed cigarettes during times of extreme duress. When I felt so tired from the trip down and so heavy with loss that I thought I could sleep, I realized it wouldn't happen soon because the cigarette "buzz" set my nerves on the outer rim of their edge. *Why don't you just go in there and have a glass of vodka, Molly?* It was years since I had had a drink of hard liquor. I knew the statistics. One in four women whose fathers were alcoholic fell prey to the disease.

The bleak and depressing apartment closed in around me and I lost any sense of being separate from it. I couldn't let this place rub off on me. But I began to feel dirty and used like some hooker he might have picked up on the street. The filth stirred uncomfortable memories—of the women I saw Dad hanging out with in Bristol, of the degrading effects of alcohol on his appearance. Before he moved to Florida, he looked like a wino and a homeless person.

No good memories came to my rescue. I sank into a quagmire. I couldn't exhale completely. This emotional claustrophobia was shaping itself into a whopper of an anxiety attack. I so wished that someone would come and save me from the taint of Dad's life.

Around two o'clock in the morning, I was still wandering around the apartment. I'd been through just about every emotion in my closet. First, sadness that he was gone. Then relief that he was gone. I relived the time I cleaned out Dad's duplex after Julia's cancer got the best of her; how I helped him move to a smaller, less expensive apartment when his income dwindled; how I helped him pack up to move down here.

The morning that he drove his old clunker out of Bristol with a U-Haul truck attached to the rear, I breathed a sigh as deep as China. I wanted to run downtown and kiss every person on the street, to swan dive off the high dive at the local pool or, better yet, hang glide off Grandfather Mountain. And I was afraid of heights. I prayed he would make it all the way down to Florida without a problem but I didn't really care. He was gone. My vigil was over. In the days and weeks that came after Dad left town, a slow reckoning came to me. I had not ever seen my father happy except when he was married to Julia. She was his love, his equal in intelligence and sensibility, and his drinking buddy. After she died, I had fallen back into my unhealthy role of caretaker. Though I tried to escape into a time-intensive business, I was not able to rest knowing that Dad was alone, desperate for money, drunk. I spent as much time trying not to think about him as I thought about him. He shadowed my days relentlessly. So when Aunt Sis sent him a check to help him relocate, she effectively took him off my watch. I felt a lightness of being, a slow deflation of stale air, permission to breathe and engage in my life fully.

Here in his apartment, stumbling from exhaustion, I started to cry. *God, why have you deserted me? This isn't fair. I don't deserve to be in this place. Where are you when I need you? Why do I feel that this is all I'm worth? That I deserve this? What's wrong with me that I can't ask for what I need most?* Help, basic comfort, love. I wanted to get this over with. I wanted to close the chapter on my dad. Was it possible to move on? I had no choice except to believe in myself.

I stretched out on Dad's bed and let my tears carry me off to a fitful sleep. Around 5:00 in the morning, I woke up to the grind of metal on metal as a train raced by the apartment building. The sound and vibration were so loud that I imagined it to be Dad snoring beside me. I jumped up abruptly and flew into the wall beside the bed. My nose and chin hurt enough to be broken but there was no blood. Again the eerie unreality of the situation closed in on me. The room felt cold now. And there was a foggy presence moving beside and then above the bed. It was Dad. I knew it. He was there. And I knew he would come. But somehow I couldn't speak to him. I was too confused about where I was, how I felt—still distrusting my perceptions. As if scripted and memorized, I yelled out, "Dad, I don't want you to be here. Please go away. This is hard enough. I can't make myself feel love for you right now. I'm sorry. I'm too angry. I'm too alone. You're scaring me, and I can't breathe. If you're gonna haunt me, why don't you say something!" Then as if the air went out of the balloon, the room became still. Dad left me alone with the dregs of his life. And I would not feel his presence again.

Unable to go back to sleep, I got up, took a shower, and started the great excavation in the living room where the one light bulb barely illuminated the space. Somewhere in my head I heard the words: *This too shall pass. There is a finite amount of work to do. You made it through the night, get busy.* And, for the first time, I began to relax and let myself down into the mess and detritus of the apartment.

After bringing me breakfast, Jay drove me to the crematory in Fort Walton where we made arrangements for Dad's ashes to be delivered to my house in Bristol. We planned to hold a memorial and place them in the columbarium at Emmanuel Episcopal Church, in a vault beside Julia.

After that, Tom and Jay left to play golf. I got back to work, sorted and tossed and smoked, sorted and tossed and made trips to the dumpster. In one box, I found a trove of old family photographs. I sorted those too—some for me, some for Jay, some for Laura. There were two small identical china plates that I knew belonged to Julia. I wrapped them for my girls. And every now and then, I cried.

I worked through lunch and started sorting Dad's paperwork. I found the important stuff: his social security card, his discharge papers from the military, his driver's license, and his dog tag. I stumbled across a file marked IRS. It held a letter dated July 28, 1994. It read:

In re: Lien on bank account
1. The individual above captioned, and the unincorporated business filed for bankruptcy on Oct. 9, 1992. . . .
2. The captioned has no assets beyond the balance in the sole bank account against which lien was filed, scant personal possessions within a rented 3-bedroom apartment

plus equity in a 1979 model automobile against which a lien, attributable to a bank failure, continues to exist.

To emphasize:

* I have no bank checking or savings accounts.

* I have no stocks, bonds, insurance equity or collateral of any sorts.

* I am owed no debts.

Therefore, I respectfully request immediate cancellation of the above mentioned lien. I do not have money for food, I cannot pay rent due within the next few days and I am out of prescription medicines considered essential to my survival. I, Harris J. Fields, certify upon oath the correctness of information submitted.

Oh . . . my. How utterly heartbreaking. Tears welled up and spilled over and onto the page. I cried for Dad and I cried for me. This letter, so raw, came from the pen of my father at perhaps his lowest point. He would feel such shame if he knew I found it and more, if he knew I exposed it to anyone else. But the language was that of a man who was sober—sober and honest about his circumstances. Beneath it all, I could find dignity in that.

I thought back to 1994 and remembered that I was consumed by the demands of my business, Book Ends. My small, independent bookstore housed in an aging 1920s building in downtown Bristol was where I could be found six days a week ordering, shelving, selling. Dad created my logo and helped me get the word out before we opened in May 1991. His business was hanging on by a thread; the graffiti was on the wall. In the next year, he showed up at odd times, disheveled and anxious. He asked to borrow money, five hundred dollars, a thousand—depending on how desperate he was at that time of the month.

At first, I took money from my husband's and my joint account. There was no fluff in the bookstore coffers. I was plowing everything I earned back into the books. But, before long, I became too embarrassed to approach my husband for more money. One day in the spring of 1994, I saw Dad coming. He was unshaven, his clothes were wrinkled and shoddy. He had on an old trench coat, wet from the rain. As soon as I could get to him, I drew him to the back of the store and said, "Dad, you can't come here to the bookstore anymore to ask me for money. Please, hear what I'm saying." He turned away without speaking. He walked down the aisle and out the front door. That was the last time he came to Book Ends, and the last time he asked me for money.

☙❧

When Jay got back to Dad's apartment, he helped me for a while, but I could tell by his quiet and sad expression that the work was taking him down. At least, that was the excuse I gave myself for wanting to forge ahead alone. At 9:00 p.m., we called it quits, close enough to being finished that we could make our flight the following afternoon. When I climbed into Dad's bed the second night, I felt beat up as if I had been in the boxing ring all day with three Amazon women. Every muscle ached. Odd pieces of furniture stood like ghosts in the living room. The apartment was as devoid of spirit as Dad's unresponsive body had been the day before. I had lifted, sorted, tossed, cried, remembered, until I was wrung out of energy and emotion. Once asleep, I stayed that way until morning light.

Three weeks later, we held Dad's memorial service. Jay drove over to Bristol from his home in Asheville. Laura and Scott came from Cookeville, Tennessee, for the day. Aunt Sis, Uncle Bill, and Aunt Lib drove in from North Carolina. The church was half full and most of the people there were old family friends. My mother arrived late and sat in the back pew. Jay read from the letter that Dad wrote to the family from North Africa during the war. Some people wept. Many, who didn't know my father as a young man, saw him in a different light and understood our profound sadness. I watched as Dad's ashes were deposited in a drawer in the enclosed garden of the columbarium. I thought I was finished with my father.

CHAPTER SEVENTEEN

History

When I moved to Asheville in 2001 and contemplated how ill prepared I was to deal with grief, to care for the terminally ill, I signed up for hospice training. A year later I was recruited as a trainer to set up programs in faith communities. My job involved the organization of care teams who would provide much-needed assistance to families of the dying. Before long, I found myself in a situation that brought me face to face with unresolved issues.

A retired clergyman, lean, stooped, balding, with kind eyes and a Connecticut accent, asked me to visit the Church of the Advocate—a spiritual oasis for the homeless. He wanted me to assess the community and help determine whether or not we could establish a care team there. He thought we could find a way to mobilize some of the "regulars."

"Most of the people who come to the Advocate are so marginalized and have worked so hard just to survive from one day to the next that they would not be available for teamwork, but there are about thirty regulars," he told me. "Betty, for example, has a police scanner and a cell phone. I think she would be willing to be a contact. She could let us know when someone gets arrested, beaten up, falls ill or dies, and that happens more often than you might think."

"How do most of these people become homeless?"

"Most of them are underprivileged to begin with. But some are college-educated folks. Things like alcohol, drugs, and abuse bring people to the streets. With those things in mind, do you think we can start to talk about this informally at the Advocate, to see if there's any interest in the circle?"

"Not having been there," I told him, "I don't know enough to tell you, and the only way for me to find out is to attend services for a while, pay close attention, and get to know some of the people. I don't think it will work if we try to impose a structure on a group like this. My guess is that they will only agree to teamwork if they craft it themselves. But I've gotta tell you, I'm not sure I can do this."

Bill didn't say anything, but waited for me to go on. I told him that my father had been a serious, abusive alcoholic, that he lost nearly everything he had—his family, his job, his health. Homelessness was barking at his apartment door along with the IRS. I had some fear about getting involved.

"Fair enough. Take some time to think about it and if you don't come, we'll understand."

Several weeks passed before I could work up the nerve to follow through. On a bright, sunny Sunday, I approached the grounds of Trinity Church. I looked at the disheveled and grimy men, both white and African American, leaning against the building and forced myself to walk past them into the dedicated space of the Advocate.

Inside the basement room lit with candles and sunshine from the casement windows, I spied a large cross made of lashed-together pieces of driftwood. Under it were two signs that looked like they were painted out on a farm: "Love One Another" and "Delighted in You." A poster read, "He who conceals his disease cannot expect to be cured." The chairs in the front half of the room were arranged in a large circle with the altar at one end. I found an empty seat next to my friend Bill, and sat down. In the back of the room were round tables where some men—rough, dirty, disheveled, and downtrodden—sat. It seemed that they couldn't tolerate the closeness and intimacy. I watched them drink coffee and look down—no eye contact—some without a flicker of light in their eyes.

The young rector, Brian, began the service saying, "Please say your first name, offering yourself, a child of God." This was my first cue that the twelve steps were woven into the liturgy. So there I was, Molly, just Molly. Just a person, like all the others. There was no hierarchy of personage.

Brian introduced the parable of the lost sheep and asked if anyone wanted to comment. Karen, a young woman still in her twenties who came to the Advocate with her friend Joe and their baby, Ashley, had bipolar disorder and addiction problems. She responded in a quiet voice. "God wants to enfold us all, whether we sin or not." After a month of attending services, I saw Karen hobble in with a broken leg. She told me that she had a fit of paranoia one night and jumped from the second story of her apartment building with Ashley in her arms. She lost custody. When she poured out her story to me, I felt her shame, her complete devastation, and cried with her.

After Karen's response to the parable, Thomas, a Vietnam veteran, began to tell his story of serving in the war. "I was shipped overseas in 1968 when my boy was just three year old. I seen things over there you wouldn't believe if I told you. I got my leg shot real bad and started doin' heroin to keep the pain down. When I got back home, they weren't no parade, nobody cared that I went. My wife left me so I didn't have no place to live. Now my boy's growed up and he tries to get me to stay at his place but I won't do it. I don't want no home now. This fuckin' country used me up. I'm livin' out there in the woods by the river." At this point, I became anxious and uncomfortable.

Then Brian offered communion and though I have persistently refused to believe that I will get sick drinking from the common cup, I took the bread and dipped it in the wine, afraid I would pick up a bug, a serious illness, AIDS, filth, poverty, paranoia, delusions of grandeur, hunger, depravity, homelessness. What if I turned out to be like these people, like my father?

The service began to come to a close. Brian stood before us, his hands in front of his heart, fingers doing push-ups against each other. I started to think about getting out of there—leaving before the end so I didn't have to talk to anyone—but before I could move, Brian stepped in front of the cross and we all joined hands for the benediction:

My brothers and sisters, the world is now too dangerous and
too beautiful for anything but love. So may God take your
minds and think through them, may God take your hands
and feet and work through them, may God take your hearts
and set them on fire.

The room became silent for a few seconds, and then I noticed
that more men and women were rustling and shuffling into the
back of the room—moving toward the kitchen. A couple of them
appeared to be staggering and swaying. The newcomers appeared
to be there for a free cup of coffee, a few cookies, a handout.

Without making eye contact with Bill or Brian, I walked across
the circle, down the hall, and out into the sunshine. I headed for
my car feeling speechless and teary, and needing to get to the
safety and comfort of my own home as quickly as I could.

March 2008

Two years have passed since the family secret eclipsed all other
distractions in my life except for teaching and the births of two
grandchildren. I had focused almost entirely on finding answers,
traveling back and forth to Mississippi. After all I had uncovered,
I still wasn't certain what happened that night or why. Why was I
still possessed by this story? What did it mean?

I dropped by Jay's house one Sunday after church to share
some letters I had found. He lived in Kenilworth near downtown
Asheville. "Grungy-cool" would be a good descriptor of the fading
red craftsman bungalow with its original woodwork, windows,
and kitchen. White flower boxes on the front were stenciled in
faded green ginko leaves. His furniture was late-divorce (an event
that had occurred twenty-five years ago). And the door frames
and walls of his office (which had windows on three sides) were
adorned with Jay's excellent photographs and watercolors, some
Rumi poetry, and an odd *New Yorker* cartoon. Always casual and
unruffled, he read through the letters, handed them back to me

and then asked, "Did I ever show you the drawings Dad made of his imaginary house in Scotland?"

Dad was no artist but he had created a pencil drawing of a hillside with a small red building set back among trees. There was a drive that circled the front. With blue magic marker he had drawn a creek around the property. The following description accompanied the drawing:

The road follows the creek bed for a mile out of the village. At that point, the creek loops outward from the road, leaving a level semi-circle for one-half mile before rejoining the road. That semi-circle, encompassing 12 acres, is mine! In the middle of a long, straight stretch which provides visibility in both directions is my driveway framed by field stone fences. The driveway descends gently to the surface of the land which falls away on the backside some 20 feet to the stream, gurgling through stones carefully spaced to provoke a constant oral reminder of its presence.

The house is in the midst of a small grove of old trees which almost mask it from the road. Its rear terrace traverses the entire length of the structure, ending on a bluff above the creek.

The house is old. The ancient bricks have faded to a soft pink. Four chimneys, serving eight fireplaces soar over the metal roof, painted a weathered grayish green. A brick terrace stretches the entire length of the front. A fanlight crosses the huge old original door. Windows are from floor to ceiling.

Despite its size, it is a working farm. Sheep graze on approximately half of the acreage. A kitchen garden, cornfield, an orchard and a tiny plot for my tobacco allotment occupy the remainder. It is snug, undemanding and my overriding joy.

A floor plan followed with a drawing of the exterior. I studied his heavy black, blocky, masculine handwriting, his primitive drawings, and wondered what caused him to want to escape across the sea and into another, solitary life.

❦

I sat down on the faded and sagging blue floral sofa and glanced around Jay's house. The screenless windows were open with a coolish breeze flowing through. Miles purred and wound his way around my legs so I gave him a gentle stroke. A vase of fresh hydrangeas adorned the mantle across from me. And Thelonious Monk filled the background with a sonorous riff on an old melody. Jay, like my father, had the ability to enhance the moment with sensory delight. He was mellow, relaxed, and pensive.

"How did you react to this when Dad gave it to you?"

"I thought it was neat that he could conjure up something like this . . . really interesting. And I thought about what a voluminous reader he was, how he loved a long saga like Michener wrote. Do you remember that he had a similar fascination for sailing?"

"No. I must have been out of the house then."

"He dreamed about sailing the intracoastal waterway. He studied sailing diagrams, read books on sailing. Rather than putting the boat together piece by piece with his own hands, he did it all in his head. He put the sail up and brought it down—in his mind—worked the rigging, navigated the deep waters."

"I do remember that he had some sailing books stacked up in his living room."

"I have to think that his alcoholism kept him pinned down in a way. I think it was kind of a virtue to get to places the way he did."

"Do you see any connection between these imaginary worlds and the fact that he may have killed two men?"

"After that incident occurred, he had to rationalize it away."

"Compartmentalize it?"

"Well, if you want to know the truth, I think there were more horrific events in his childhood, like the death of his father and

living with an overbearing mother, that affected him more pro-
foundly. He knew it was a horrible thing, and he probably felt
sorry that it happened, but once it was over, it was over and he
decided to move beyond it."

I thought the words "felt sorry" were minimal and diminished
the terror Dad must have felt when the smoke lifted in the tavern that night and afterwards when he was arrested, charged, and
jailed. I would imagine that his faculties of denial and rational-
ization and even his false sense of "rightness" for what he had
done could not have overcome his alarm until weeks, maybe
months, later. That his father died when he was a young lad, that
his mother overpowered him—these things could not be com-
pared to the aggression he himself displayed, nor to the sight of
the bodies of two human beings in whose deaths he was deeply
involved. Yet, Dad had not confided in anyone about what really
happened. He had left no written testament. Nor, it seems, did he
have a moment of purgative, cathartic release.

"You know, as I read through his letters and think back, it is so
clear how much he loved his family and how proud he was of his
heritage. Remember the print he designed and produced when he
was in advertising—the one about Ashland?"

"Yeah, but I haven't looked at it in a long time."

"Clearly Dad inherited a love of land."

Later, when I got home, I went to my study, found the old
print and read the words surrounded in cotton blossoms: "As
the planter prospered he expanded his tillable acreage by carv-
ing from the virgin forests new fields to be put to the plow. Huge
cypress and oaks felt the saw, lesser trees were dropped and
pools which had existed for time unremembered were drained
by intricate systems of ditches. The trees were mule-tugged into
huge pyres and bonfires kindled, sending flames hundreds of feet
into the sky. As the fires burned for weeks on end, white ashes
collected on the ground, covering these fields like a deep winter's snow. Thus the planter named these acres ASHLAND. There
are 572 of them and they have borne that name to yet this day.
1867–1975."

Jay took a sip from a chipped mug of hot tea and said, "Molly, when I was real young, Dad said, 'You never have to worry about holding your head up with kings, queens, and monarchs because of your background.' And I never have. I'm comfortable with just about anybody."

Dad never said that to me. Instead, I remembered how crippling his words could be. Mom told me that when Jay was getting ready to leave for Woodbury, Dad said, "Son, you've never done anything right in your whole life." She was infuriated and when she told me, I was appalled. Dad was proud, sometimes generous, and also sometimes hard, very hard.

☙❧

Later that day, I returned to my photograph albums and piles of papers and letters, trying to find the good, the loving parts of my father. Now that the intrigue of the secret had begun to wear off, and Dad had been dead for eight years, my anger was fading and my heart opened to intense sadness.

I located one of the many journals I'd kept over the years, the one I used when the bookstore was failing, and I was floundering, trying to decide how best to use my gifts, energy, and resources. Jay sent me a notice of an Artist's Way workshop being held in Asheville. The course was designed by Julia Cameron, who based the curriculum on her book. I signed up and drove over once a week, searching for something—I didn't know what. One of our assignments was to interview members of our family of origin about their lives. I had spoken with Mom, Jay, Uncle Tom, and Dad. By then, Dad had moved to Florida so I sent him a list of questions and asked that he write me back with his answers. What are your strengths? "I am not a strong person. I have been spared the crucible of deprivation, tragedy and ill-health which strengthen character. I am blessed/cursed with an extraordinary ability to see all manner of shades of grey. Thus my reactions are seldom with staunch conviction." Maybe that characteristic made him a good reporter.

What are your weaknesses? "My desire for peace and concord. I shun verbal confrontations until my patience is exhausted, then I overreact." I had seen that happen too many times. What are your greatest achievements? "Three exceptional children who are, in turn, producing exceptional children." What do you fear most? "Disgrace. Helplessness. Strangely enough, loneliness is not one of my fears." I paused several minutes after reading the word—disgrace—and wondered what was the genesis of that fear in him. What could have happened to him or what could he have done that would dishonor him, unless it was the despicable act of losing control to the extent that he could take another life . . . or two. It is clear to me now that once exonerated, Dad put aside the disgrace he may have felt at bringing the family into a scandalous incident.

What dreams were you unable to realize? "To be a successful, professional writer. To have worked on the *New York Times*." Any failures? "Yes. Business failures. I elected a path-finding career and failed to get out of the forest."

That brought up a memory from high school. Mom's derisive comments to Dad about money—the lack of it—caused me to feel sorry for him. One night when we were talking, he expressed chagrin at not having provided more adequately for us. I thought about it and replied, "Dad, I appreciate the way you have followed your heart into creative work. It takes courage to do that and not many people can say that they do what they love." He handed me a copy of a brochure his agency had just produced for the newly renovated Paramount Theatre in Bristol. It was slick and appealing and promoted the history and careful restoration of the art deco building. I told him how much I loved the piece.

In his written answers to my questions, he was, at least, honest with himself and with me. But though he had vision, an eye for design, and the crisp enthusiasm of an ad man, he was conditioned by the times in which he lived. Mid-twentieth-century mores in his part of the world allowed for racial inequality, injustice, and entitlement. Those values were mired in Dad's blood and though he became less vocal about them as he aged, they were still lurking underneath a polished exterior.

In the same box where I found my journals, there was a memo that Dad wrote to "loved ones and friends" when my first child was born. In it he wrote about visiting my newborn infant just hours after her arrival at 7:50 a.m. January 4, 1975, at Piedmont Hospital in Atlanta. He described her chubby cheeks, her "cupid's bow mouth," her contented nature, her dexterity and strength.

But he ended the letter with this: "Whitney's actual presence strengthens a grandfather's already considerable sense of the life forces moving through the misty past to grandparents he knew and loved, now to his own grandchild he knows and loves.

"The span of this ken is 150 years and covers three-quarters of the life of our nation, yet is but the bat of an eyelash in eternity."

Reading these words at a time when I felt stymied and flummoxed opened up the possibility that there might be some new understanding to be gained from widening my perspective to take in the generations before Dad. I pulled out a thick roll of freezer paper and made a new and more detailed time line for the family. Once again I sifted through the many versions I had heard of what happened the night Dad or Bill killed two men. Aunt Sis's rendition included a detail unlike anyone else's. She said that when Dad and Tom entered the Pan Am station, someone turned off the lights, immersing everyone there in darkness. I wondered how Dad (or Bill) could have fired his weapon so accurately if he couldn't see. How was someone else able to "bull's-eye" Tom's left shoulder—in the dark? It wasn't until many months later that I discovered another barroom episode, the details of which were appropriated into the Pan Am story.

My great-grandparents Harris and Martha had thirteen children while growing a booming farming business and coming to own twenty-five hundred acres of good cotton-growing land. In 1903, my grandfather's older brother, Jesse (Dad's namesake), was shot to death in a local tavern by a German immigrant named Will Lang. The *Deer Creek Pilot* carried the story.

Jesse Fields killed by W. M. Lang

Our community was shocked and saddened Sunday
morning by the report that W. M. Lang had shot and mortally wounded H. J. Fields, Jr., in a difficulty at Anguilla Saturday night. Later this report was confirmed, with the further
statement that young Fields had been taken to Vicksburg for
medical treatment. All that medical science could do was
without avail and on Monday morning he breathed his last.

So many rumors are abroad as to the unfortunate occur-
rence that we refrain from trying to give a correct statement
of the causes that led up to it, but await the investigation of
the affair by the grand jury, to which, by mutual consent, the
case was referred, and Mr. Lang was bound over in the sum
of $5,000.

Jesse Fields was a native of Sharkey County and had
passed his entire life here, where he had a host of friends,
who sorrow for his untimely death, and deeply sympathize
with his bereaved relatives.

Subsequent research in circuit court documents didn't mention the case, which suggests that they didn't indict Lang. I can
only imagine the heartache that my family felt when Jesse died
such a violent death at twenty-four years of age. Thomas was not
prepared for the toll this took on his mother, Martha Katherine.
She died the very next year at fifty-five, leaving her husband with
six grown children and a lovely new two-story home on the Deer
Creek. Harris, who was sixty-two years old in 1904, didn't sleep a
single night in the house he'd built for Martha. Thomas, twenty-
two, was a bachelor.

If Aunt Sis had heard this story of a previous barroom shoot-
out or some part of it and had mistakenly woven it into my father's
tale, then Dad had to have heard this oral history too. No, the
lights were not shut out on him the night Simon and David died,
but he had to have known that bars were dangerous places where
people sometimes met untimely deaths. His namesake was the

same age Dad was when he entered the Pan Am that night. Proving guilt or innocence was difficult, if not impossible. Murderers walked away from their misdeeds without consequence. And families only spoke of these incidents in hushed voices, if at all.

☙❧

On January 15, 1911, Simon Toombs was born. At the time of his birth, Harris was sixty-nine and Thomas was twenty-nine. Father and son were no doubt farming, ginning, banking, and, according to several sources, drinking. It is quite possible that Leana, Simon's mother, had caught the attention of one of the Fields men. She was a midwife, frequently in the homes of young families, maybe even helping to birth two of Harris's grandchildren born in 1909 and 1910. If Charles Weissinger's story holds truth, Simon could have been an offspring of either Thomas or his father. It is hard to imagine that both men remained abstinent those seven years between Martha's death and Simon's birth. In reality, there might have been other children fathered during that time or before. Thomas was younger but his father had proven to be virile and prolific.

Simon and his brother, Shelby, were raised in Leana's home, taught to stay away from white children—told not to pick a fight with one because it might get them killed—and they learned that the only safe place to express themselves was there, with their family, or at church.

In 1919, Harris, who was staring down the final years of his life, divided the land and gave my grandfather, then thirty-seven, Ashland. Tom was already an accomplished farmer, a vice president at the Bank of Anguilla, and still a hardcore bachelor. A look at the deed book listing conveyances into and out of Harris's and Thomas's holdings between 1911 and 1946 reveals no legal transactions involving Simon. If either of them provided for an out-of-wedlock, African American son, it would have been in the form of an oral bequest. We simply cannot know if that gift was made.

❦

Two years later Thomas met Rebekah Blanks, nineteen, who had recently come to the local elementary school to teach expression. Rebekah, who would become my mamaw, came from a family that had lived in Tennessee until they moved to Houston, Mississippi, to lumber. They purchased an old hotel there. Uncle Tom and Aunt Sis both told me that their mother was attractive as a young woman, that she had lovely auburn hair and a beautiful voice. She was highly successful at coaxing people into buying war bonds during World War I. When she was eighteen, her parents sent her to the Cincinnati Conservatory. After that she was hired by the Anguilla elementary school. She loved teaching speech and went right to work directing the children in short plays.

Soon Mamaw caught Tom's eye and they fell in love. For their marriage, they traveled by train to Black Mountain, North Carolina, where her sister had a house not twenty miles from my own home. The whole Blanks family convened for the wedding at the Methodist church. During that union/reunion, one of Mamaw's brothers spied the "For Sale" sign on the Riverby Inn. In the next year, the Blanks family pulled out of Houston and moved to Swannanoa.

In 1922, my father was born in the Ashland homeplace. His baby book has black-and-white photographs of his nurse, and of Marsh, the house girl, John, the "yard boy," and Frances, the cook. There is also a photo of a chubby little boy, not a year old, wearing a smock and leggings, sitting on his father's lap. Dad leans back into his father's shoulder and is supported by strong hands with interlaced fingers around his knees. Tom is wearing a tweed suit with tie—his head lowered, a slight smile, warm, loving eyes, a deep brow and the aura of a kind and contented man—dignified would not be too strong a word for him. His proud chin, replicated in each of his offspring, is a defining feature. This was a man I would love to have known. He appears to have had a quiet nature, and though he was not celebrated in his life as his father was, for serving his country in war, he was greatly loved by all who knew him.

Rebekah gave birth to Tom, Jr., in 1924 and Bill in 1926. Then the family faced serious calamity. The great flood of the Mississippi River in 1927 forced a retreat from the Delta. Mamaw and the boys, with Aunt Mat in tow, were boated to Vicksburg and then traveled by train to Ohio. Tom stayed with his father in Anguilla. The land was utterly consumed by the raging water that spilled over the riverbanks. In his book *The Most Southern Place on Earth*, James Cobb describes the flood:

> The 1927 flood cost the lives of from 250 to 500 people and left more than 16.6 million acres and 162,000 homes under water. . . . After the flood receded, a visitor to Greenville reported that, although the water was gone, its mark remained in the form of "deeply seared scars upon the face of the fair land, and more deeply still upon the hearts and minds, and the hopes, and the very futures of the young and the old." Those who had survived the flood and struggled to rid their stench-ridden homes of mud, snakes, crawfish, and frogs took heart in the news of an extensive flood-control effort, but each new spring came in with irrepressible anxiety that this might be the year when another 'watery Armageddon' would come.

Mamaw returned to a home swept clean by laborers. Another photo in Dad's baby book was taken when her flower garden was in full bloom the next year. But fear of another flood remained. Tom's father kept his Chris-Craft outboard parked on the top of an Indian mound beside his town house in Anguilla, just in case the waters should rise again.

Tom made plans to protect his family. He hired an architect out of Louisville, Kentucky, to design the brick home that was completed in 1931 when Aunt Sis was two years old. They moved from Ashland and erected shotgun houses along an alley behind the house. Fifteen black families moved in, many with small children. Aunt Sis told me that when the winter came, Tom continued to support these families through the hard time. She said that black male laborers "would get their money at the end of the year [planting season] and they'd spend it before nightfall or they would gamble it away or they'd stab each other, so the children were starving to death." Her story, clearly based on a white, racist viewpoint and exaggeration, omits the fact that these were hard-working laborers living in poverty and oppression with the darkness and despair that accompany destitution. That's when Mamaw conceived the idea of employing the women to make bedspreads for some extra money during the cold months. "And they didn't go in and buy the stuff. I mean, she'd write in the book, 'Rosa took one African Daisy design, X amount of spools of yarn,' and that would go up against what she made when she sold the finished products. And Rosa, or whatever her name was, would get that money."

Come spring, Mamaw gave the women seed that they could plant around their houses and beautify them. She gave small cash prizes to the two or three most attractive yards. But her main goal was to somehow work against the mosquito-infested water that stood under the houses and made the children sick.

When the heat became oppressive, Tom and Rebekah loaded Dad and his sibs in the big black Buick LaSalle and drove to the North Carolina mountains. What the kids heard was, "Let's take the children up for a summer vacation at the Riverby." In truth, Mamaw's parents needed help putting dinner on the table. "Granny grew everything in the garden. She had an apple orchard and cherry trees all down the side of the mountain. People would come there once and be coming back every summer to stay for a week at twenty-five dollars. The inn's capacity was fourteen. You rang a bell, and if you wanted to have a lunch there, you could have lunch. It was kind of like a bed-and-breakfast today." When the bell rang, the children, known as the "trundle bed trash," knew that was their signal to become scarce. Sis said, "Us cousins had a glorious time going up there. We just did what they told us to do, and they were perfectly happy with us running up the mountain-side. Or we would go to the apple orchard and pick apples. And we could climb the cherry trees. If we were caught eating a cherry, we were in trouble."

Dad, Tom, Bill, and Sis scampered over the rock outcroppings, and played in the river, making things out of mud and sticks. They played the piano when no one was around, and Dad made his own brand of music on a harmonica. Occasionally they performed for the guests. One night, Dad, his brothers, and Sis marched into the dining room singing the words to "Dixie" while Sis waved a Confederate flag.

Each spring, they and their cousins created a craft project at school that would be presented to their grandmother. These gifts were placed on shelves in the music parlor. One year Dad was especially proud of his artwork. On a polished pine medallion, he had burned with his electric wood stylus his grandmother's favorite hymn.

Others, Lord, yes, others,
Let this my motto be,
Help me to live for others,
That I may live like thee.

She cried and wrapped him in her arms. "Jaybo," as they called him, had hit a home run.

When I read these and other Swannanoa stories, collected in Sis's book about the Riverby Inn, I recognized the personalities of my aunts and uncles. Dad was often the "lookout" for secret hiding places about the property. The boys often acted out boxing matches and duels. Once Uncle Bill and a cousin got into a fistfight. When their mothers responded in alarm and saw blood everywhere, they attempted to pull the boys apart. The kids erupted into laughter when the grown-ups discovered mashed cherries covering the ground.

These happy days of playing pranks, while surrounded by adults who loved them, must have been idyllic. All the while, they did not know that they may have had an older black brother growing up in Anguilla. No single aspect of this time in their lives, except for their growing sense of bravado, could foreshadow the way in which their paths would cross with his.

Because I did not know the location of the old inn, so important in my father's youth, I called the Swannanoa Valley Museum and got directions. I felt a need to walk the land and get to know it better. I wanted to recapture and resurrect a better time in my father's life.

CHAPTER EIGHTEEN

Springtime in Mississippi

May 2008

I made phone call after phone call to forensic labs in Mississippi after my friend, a district attorney in Tennessee, suggested that the scene where Simon and David were shot could still yield valuable information. She told me that a retired specialist might be available and less costly to hire. Every place I tried offered to have someone call me back but no one did.

Meanwhile, I worked to find out who currently owned the old Pan Am station. Finally, Mayor Richardson said—with certainty—that if I'd come down there, he would get me into the building. After our telephone conversation ended, full of the hope that I'd be able to gain access to the interior, I sat very still and my imagination kicked into play. I saw myself standing in the "coloreds only" room, eavesdropping on the men as they drank their whiskey, talked about their day's work, maybe boasted about their war years. I watched their faces as Dad, Bill, and Tom entered the room in a heat, determined to send the black men on their way. I felt the tension mount as age-old anger, the black men's abandonment of pride, their low self-esteem, and sense of futility combusted into harsh words. I watched the Fields men asserting themselves—first verbally, then with physical aggression—hell-bent on maintaining the caste system that had begun so many generations ago. Then, I could see David Jones reach for his pocket. Tom, who was right handed, may have had his arms lifted in self-defense or preparation to thrust forward, when he felt the sting of a bullet entering the flesh of his left shoulder.

That would have been the point when a return volley struck and mortally wounded David. At that point, everyone scattered. The Fields men chased Simon Toombs out of the building and fired multiple shots into his back. Maybe my father killed them. Maybe my uncle Bill. What mattered most to me then, and now, was that intersecting lives and countless social, economic, historical, psychological elements zinged into place in an instant. This drama could have played on a similar stage anywhere that class and privilege met with degradation and resistance.

At critical, defining moments in my own life, I have learned to stop and reflect on the wisdom of a great thinker, Albert Einstein, who said that a problem cannot be solved at the level at which it is experienced. Violence does not engender peace. My father could not perceive a higher calling when he found himself in a tragic confrontation. He had an opportunity to change course but he didn't, and racial relations in the dark heart of Mississippi took a step backwards. If only he had gone to the courthouse first, he would have discovered, as I did, that there was no record of a transfer of land to Simon Toombs.

☙❧

On the first of June, I tossed my duffle into the back of my green Subaru station wagon and left for the Delta, making it only as far as Meridian when massive black clouds unleashed a storm that threatened to hijack my car. I spent what was left of the day planning, and drove on early the next morning to meet Mr. Richardson at the mayor's office in Anguilla.

After we chatted about the mundane, Mr. Richardson asked me which building I wanted to enter. I thought he knew, but soon figured out that he had no idea. We got in his car and drove to the site that King Evans had taken me to—at which point Mr. Richardson told me that one of the Klein brothers held the deed. The problem was that Mr. Klein was out of town so we couldn't go in. To assuage my disappointment, he drove to the Gipson home, which sat on Highway 61 to the left of my grandmother's house. "Gip" was Mamaw's gin manager and right-hand man in business. Were he still alive, I would have learned a great deal from him.

Jo Anderson, Gip's daughter, now in her late seventies or early eighties, met us at the door with a broad, welcoming grin. She was friendly, jolly, and spry, and clearly a great friend of the mayor. After telling me about her grandchildren and talking with Mr. Richardson about church affairs, she asked about my project. I gave her the basic details, and with a smile she said she just didn't recall anything about it. She must have felt it best to sidetrack the conversation because she changed the subject to the new family with ten children preparing to move into Greenfields, next door. It was my turn to smile, knowing that my grandmother would be happy with that news too. The home place would soon be throbbing to life with the energy of small children, the joys and hardships of family life.

ঙ৾৹

As this vision shifted into my heart, I remembered the best Christmas of my childhood, that time of life when all holidays are magical. The year was 1957. Jay was eleven, Laura, two, and I was eight. Mamaw had invited us, as well as our aunts and uncles and cousins, to her house for the festivities. Our old green Chevy wagon was loaded with brightly wrapped and ribboned boxes and a nest of suitcases. We left Knoxville early that day for the warmth of the Mississippi Delta. The road trip stretched out into flatter land and the drone of the engine added monotony. In those days, the car seat had not become a necessity, so my pesky little sister, Laura, roamed the car, climbing back and forth over the bench seat to invade Jay's and my territory, then crawling back up front to Mom's lap. She was getting under my skin.

Somewhere in the middle of Tennessee, Dad pulled into a service station to gas up the car. Back then, an attendant would actually look under the hood, wash the windows, and pump the gas. Then Dad corralled us and we headed back onto the southern route, a two-lane road. Not a mile from the gas station, calamity struck when the hood of the car, not securely fastened, flew up and back at sixty miles an hour, wrapping itself around the windshield. Mom screamed the second she looked down, through the slit of window just above the dash, and saw a semi heading toward us in the opposite lane. Dad, the pilot, maintained command of the car, white-knuckled hands gripping the steering wheel. Dad couldn't see what was in front of him, so he slowed down gradually, not overreacting to the oncoming danger, and edged our car onto the shoulder of the road. The giant truck created a back draft and a roar that registered fear in all of us. That part of our trip would become "the" story we would tell our aunts and uncles.

Just as our car entered the circular drive, Mamaw threw open the front door and charged toward us, arms wide open. Jay, Laura, and I scrambled from the car like white mice let loose from a cage. Mamaw hugged all three of us at one time, so happy that we were there.

The dining room table was set for nine adults. The glass-top tables on the side porch and in the breakfast nook were set for thirteen grandchildren. Jo and Aunt Mat were busy in the hot, steamy kitchen. It took a half hour to unpack the car, nestle our gifts under the giant Christmas tree, and greet everyone. Soon the adults were deep into their toddies and the kids were running helter-skelter about the lawn. I sought out Aunt Mat in the kitchen and asked if I could go with her to her one-room house. She took me by the hand and led me along the alley to her front door. We entered and my eyes traveled immediately to the wall beside her iron bed. It was covered in red, green, and gold Christmas cards—some from her church community, some from her children, now scattered as far away as California. There was no Christmas tree. There were no gifts. But her voice lifted in excitement as she showed me each card and shared information about the sender.

After supper we settled down for stories and games and then found our way into the upstairs bedroom where thirteen pallets abutted each other the length of the room. Sometime in the wee hours of the morning, I was awakened by yelling. Uncle Tom had stepped into an icy cold shower. We had depleted the last few drops of hot water.

The following morning, just as the sun began to peek above the horizon, we rousted our parents out of bed and scrambled down the long staircase, some of us sliding on the polished mahogany banister. Each family had a corner set aside for Santa Claus to arrange our presents. Jay, Laura, and I found our stash in the dining room. I only remember that my favorite gift came from my other grandparents, Mam and Joe. It was a small electric organ with no more than twenty-five keys. It had a songbook and a long cardboard diagram that was color coded and soon I was able to pick out "Joy to the World." I was so in love with my new toy that I hardly left its side and froze when my cousins came to play it.

Jay was given a motorized airplane with a wingspan of about twenty-four inches. After lunch we assembled on the lawn to watch Dad fire it up for liftoff—he was ready to teach Jay all he knew about flying. The plane ran along the ground, rose about twenty feet into the air, and then began to circle the expanse of the yard. Jay was beside himself with pleasure and anticipation, itching to get his hands on the instrument box. But we watched in horror as Dad flew the plane too wide. Its wing caught in the magnolia tree. The motor died, and like an unfortunate bird shot down on a dove hunt, the plane came loose and fell with increasing speed to the ground. Wings broke off. The propeller bent. It was dead. Because I was so enraptured with my gift, I felt crushing sadness for Jay. He never got to enjoy his Christmas present.

♾

While Mayor Richardson drove me around the town, we talked.

"I just noticed that there is a motel between Anguilla and Rolling Fork. I could have been staying there instead of driving back and forth to Yazoo City."

He answered, "Oh . . . you don't want to stay there. You'd come out the next morning and there'd be no tires."

I left his office disappointed and drove to Rolling Fork, determined to sweep the library for any stray bits of history or references to the shooting. But I found myself absorbed in Mississippi lore and the great tradition of the blues minstrels.

Early the following morning I phoned Inez. She seemed glad to hear from me but sounded weak after losing her leg because of poor circulation. "The doctors are waiting for me to heal a bit more before they give me a prosthesis." She said she was sorry she wouldn't get to see me this trip, but we promised to stay in touch. Her voice was like dew on the grass during a dry spell. I felt grateful that the door remained open when so many others had slammed shut.

When I drove into Anguilla later that morning, I noticed again the water tower with the town motto: Courage to Change. How ironic that seemed, yet it was possible that this community had the right idea. Move on to the next thing. I felt a nudge in my side. Time to let go, gather it all in, and then let it go.

I stopped at the Pan Am station, parked, and walked through broken beer bottles, weeds, and trash to the side of the building where there were two sets of casement windows, full of broken panes. Since the front door was boarded up, I could only inspect from outside. The building was full of junk. The ceiling was falling in. There was an old truck parked on one side, old tires strewn everywhere. I saw that there were several rooms, but the clutter made it impossible to "see" the building as it had been in '46. Maybe a forensic person could have sussed out the scene, but I doubted it. The building was in such sad shape and had, for many years, sat abandoned as a dumping site. It just didn't have anything to offer me.

Pat Thrasher was hard at work at the Sharkey County Courthouse when I got there. We chatted briefly, and then I meandered through the shelves and tabletops of books. I was drawn to the circuit court case documents. Why hadn't we looked at them before? There it was, the clerk's report of Dad's hearing. State of Mississippi vs. H. J. Fields. The judge had ordered that the defendant be discharged on the twenty-seventh day of February, 1947. The clerk's report stated that the "Grand Jury had ignored an indictment in this case after investigation and returned no indictment against this defendant." At last I knew with finality that no justice would have come to the murderer of a black man or two in 1946.

I needed to be in touch with the Toombs family again so I phoned Rose. She was at home in Anguilla and the first words out of her mouth, spoken with tenderness, were, "And how are you doing with all of this now?" I almost cried. We talked about her health. Now on oxygen due to sleep apnea and poor circulation, she was still making trips to Greenville to help Inez convalesce. We talked about her family one more time. She told me that Leana and Shelby, Simon's mother and father, had five boys and one daughter, Mary. Aaron was the oldest. Willie was Rose and Inez's dad. There was John, Simon, and Bill. All dead now. She didn't know anything about Simon's marriage to Mary Jones because she was too young when he came back from the war. She recalled that Mary Toombs was called "Aunt Mae" and that she was a midwife like her mother. Before we hung up, she said, "May God bless us and keep us until we talk again." I felt as close to her, and to Inez, as to any family member. Their kindness exceeded the responses I got from my blood relatives, who were too mired in their own versions of the story, too defensive and fearful, to imagine what this could mean to me, to all of us.

Without looking back, I left Rolling Fork late that afternoon for Vicksburg, where I planned to meet Dad's cousin the following day. My body relaxed into the seat of the car, comfortable and easy. I knew that my journeys to the Delta had come to an end, and that I would have the time and freedom to process everything I had learned when I was back home in my office. The excavation was over. I called Jay to let him know that I was kicking the Anguilla dust off my feet. I didn't feel that I belonged there any more. He sympathized and said, "There's a bigger picture here." He was referring to the history, culture, and racial dynamics at play in Mississippi and other parts of the country in the mid-twentieth century. According to Jay, Dad was trapped in a cultural web of historic proportion—a conflicted moment in time—just on the cusp of change. Between World War II and the start of the Civil Rights Movement, men and women of both races became polarized, dug in their heels. My father was not enlightened enough to be fully humanized, to buck the old order in favor of a more just society. I could agree with Jay that yes, all could be forgiven. I knew he was right, but I didn't believe that all could be or should be forgotten.

⚬⚬

Homer Greer, his wife, Connie, and their daughter, Laura, met me for lunch at an upscale gourmet dining room in downtown Vicksburg. Laura presented me with a copy of the family genealogy chart, one that I already had, but I was touched. Homer, very quiet, just listened as his chatty wife told stories about Aunt Laura, my dad's favorite aunt. My sister was named after her, as was Homer's daughter. He offered up only one story about Dad. When we still lived in Anguilla in the late '40s, Homer and Dad took the local Boy Scout den to Vicksburg for a parade. Dad made a parachute out of his handkerchief and pocket knife and floated it above the pack of boys.

I waited until after our meal before I asked about the shooting. Homer lowered his head and mumbled that he just didn't remember what happened and had not heard the story discussed in the family. When I told them that Aunt Sis and Aunt Lib felt I was trespassing in forbidden territory, Connie said, "I bet!" But it was becoming clear that no one in the family knew as much about the incident as I did. No one cared to find out.

Before I left them, we exchanged hugs. It had been a warm and pleasant experience that reminded me of the best part of my family's good nature. I felt blessed to have made contact with these lovely, accepting cousins, and I drove back to Asheville with a lift in my spirits.

CHAPTER NINETEEN

Reasonable Doubt

August 12, 2008

Somehow the materials I photocopied at the Rolling Fork library shuffled themselves into a tall stack of papers on my desk. When I ran across them again, I found the June 1948 issue of the *Staple Cotton Review*. It interested me because on the front page was a copy of Governor Fielding Wright's radio address to the "Negroes of Mississippi." His speech was aired eighteen months after the shooting in Anguilla. He was a Sharkey County native and a lawyer, who might have represented my father. But the reason this article jumped out of the library files and into my hands was the fact that Dad was then the editor of the *Deer Creek Pilot*, and he was a press agent for Governor Wright, who said:

> This morning I am speaking primarily to the negro citizens of Mississippi . . . We are living in troublous times and it is vital and essential that we maintain and preserve the harmonious and traditional relationship which has existed in this state between the white and colored races.
>
> It is a matter of common knowledge to all of you who have taken an interest in public affairs that in my inaugural address as governor some four months ago, I took specific issue with certain legislative proposals then being made by President Truman . . . These proposals of President Truman are concerned with the enactment of certain laws embraced within the popular term of "Civil Rights."

. . . [O]ur opposition to such legislation is that it is a definite, deliberate and outright invasion of the rights of the states to control their own affairs and meet their own duties and responsibilities. This same radical group pressing this particular proposal is also seeking to abolish separate schools in the South, separate cars on trains, separate seats in the picture shows, and every other form of physical separation between races.

Another recommendation made by the President, and one of the main objectives of the many associations claiming to represent the negroes of this nation, is the abolition of segregation. White people of Mississippi and the Southland will not tolerate such a step. The good negro does not want it. The wise of both races recognize the absolute necessity of segregation.

With all of this in mind, and with all frankness, as governor of your state, I must tell you that regardless of any recommendation of President Truman, despite any law passed by Congress, and no matter what is said to you by the many associations claiming to represent you, there will continue to be segregation between the races in Mississippi. If any of you have become so deluded as to want to enter our white schools, patronize our hotels and cafes, enjoy social equality with the whites, then true kindness and true sympathy requires me to advise you to make your homes in some state other than Mississippi.

Governor Wright goes on to say that slow and steady progress is being made on behalf of all Mississippians, regardless of color, and that it is fallacy for the government to interfere with the rights of states to proceed on this issue as they see fit.

He continued to serve as governor until 1952. Then he ran for vice president on the same ticket with Strom Thurmond as representatives of the States' Rights Party. They were defeated.

I have absolutely no doubt that my father embraced this line of thinking, as did his brothers, his sister, and my grandmother.

They held onto it with fierce resolve, and not one of them ever looked into the eyes of a black man or woman and saw a human being deserving of respect, fairness, or the right to the same freedoms, let alone the consideration, due to a brother or sister of the larger family of humanity. Knowing that Simon Toombs, a black man, might have been their blood brother would have made their staunch racist views impossible to fully maintain. It would have simultaneously become mandatory to maintain them. If Dad, Bill, and Tom knew about Simon when they went to the Pan Am station, then the same mentality, morality that sanctioned the rape of black women by white men also sanctioned these killings. It was common knowledge in the family that Thomas occasionally took a hiatus from the family, and had his house boy, John Parks, drive him to Ashland for a few days of heavy drinking. There were stories afloat that he infrequently had John take him to Memphis. This necessitated a visit to the jeweler before returning to the fold. In those days, family stood together, accepted each other, forgave acts of indecency, ignored or forgave the obvious foible. This was especially true for men. When my father was exonerated of the charge of manslaughter, whether or not he was the one that pulled the trigger, he was freed from accountability and he effectively set aside his complicity for the sake of family honor. He could go on believing as he always had.

⟡

On three separate occasions I asked my father to join Alcoholics Anonymous. The last time, I went to his office in the morning before he had a chance to dull his mind. He laughed in my face. He shamed me to the extent that I would never mention it to him again. I had no choice other than to dry the tears of disappointment, wake up to the impossibility that I might help him change, and accept the life he was choosing for himself. I had wanted my father to be a better man. I believed he had it in him.

As I write this, I can see with clear and acute vision how deeply and truly I loved Dad. The image of him that I held until I was fifty-seven years old was one that I could never quite bring into focus. Something didn't add up. I had reason enough to be wary of his moods, especially after he had descended into the bottle, and to wonder why I could not fully connect with him or trust him. But there was something else lurking in the shadows of the sepia-toned photograph of my grandmother, my aunt, Dad, and his brothers in the living room at Greenfields. Now I understand.

ॐ

My father was sometimes remote, sometimes preoccupied, distracted, sometimes lost in a good novel, sometimes ranting, sometimes arrogant and boastful, sometimes proud and dignified. Underneath his bravado was a weak man who could not allow himself to be truly intimate, who would not step forward for his children, who came to despise his wife. He was damaged and ineffectual and caught up in appearances as was my mother, but I sensed there was a deeper motivation—one linked to his acute sense of decorum and principles. He was sometimes available and willing to talk to me, yet I knew his preference for solitude. Despite his unpredictability, I felt that he had a base-level respect for me. His writerly nature made him an acute observer. He had to have sensed my awkward, gawky, insecure, and fearful approach to life, especially as it manifested in my emergence from childhood into adolescence. And he showed up at important times in my life, so he must have known that what he saw as important had become important to me too. Somehow, I developed a drive to be the best person I could be, to make him proud, to fill up the hole inside of him, inside of me.

Endowed with a well-honed sensibility, he was creative, intelligent, and appreciative of good writing, especially books that took him to another land. Toward the end of his life we traded Peter

Mayle's books about Provence. Dad loved good music as I do. He kept his radio tuned to the local classical music station. When I visited him, there was always a lively piece wafting through the environs of his home. And he loved good food, well prepared. Before Julia died, he proudly displayed his new asparagus steamer as if that was a sign that he had passed from gourmand to gourmet. These aesthetic qualities echo in my life at the same level. Maybe that is where our connection mattered most.

ૡૻૢ

The legacies of the Fields men are profound, and contain fierce, dark power. They, like many white Americans—then and now—denied an entire race of people their dignity. They, and other men like them, may have, probably did, use black women for their own sexual needs. And the Fields men participated in extinguishing two lives. To deny the significance of their deeds is to participate in the same form of self-debasement that killed my father. To forget, deny, or brush aside these facts is to fail to see the individual as a whole human being formed and molded by an era and capable of horrific deeds. To forgive is absolutely essential, especially in the confines of a family system.

August 22, 2008

The depth of the Swannanoa has reached its nadir—the lowest point since 1895. On this crisp morning the sky is the deep blue of a fall day; a gentle breeze is blowing leaves from an early drought-induced molt into the sluggish waters that run along my backyard. Rocks I have never seen before are exposed above the surface, and while the resident green heron stalks the shoreline, moving almost imperceptibly, the grating call of the kingfisher resounds when it swoops down to gullet a small fish. I sit on the back deck, waiting for a hummer to appear and poke its long beak into the sugary water I've prepared for it. The wind chime makes a sweet, lilting tune. Robber, my cat, stills his body when a squirrel clamors up the sycamore nearby.

Today I am going to search for the site of the Riverby Inn, summer playground for Dad, Tom, Bill, and Sis. According to directions obtained from the Swannanoa Valley History Museum, I should be able to reach that destination in about twenty minutes, so when I get in the car, I set the odometer, drive out of the neighborhood to Lower Grassy Branch Road and onto Highway 70 east—now a five-lane road. It is the most direct route, though it won't follow the exact contours of the river. It is the same highway that my grandmother drove, car laden with children, to the west, through Beaucatcher Tunnel into downtown Asheville, where they lunched at the S & W Cafeteria and shopped at Woolworth's.

In only ten minutes and 6.5 miles, I reach the site of the Riverby Inn. Where the white clapboard boardinghouse with green shutters once stood is a small strip shopping center and a car wash. I take in the flat, urban look of the River's Edge Center where the PSA Pharmacy, C&K Printers, and Computers for Christ are located, behind which is a double-wide, and then the land slopes down to the tree-lined banks of the Swannanoa. This site is nestled in the valley with prominent mountains rising to the south and north. No footprint of the old inn remains, only the evidence of a large yard overshadowed by a majestic weeping willow. Old Highway 70 branches off and runs back into the mountains and eventually east toward Black Mountain. Where it crosses the river, I park my car and walk out onto the bridge so that I can take in the scene of the river with the sunlight playing in the tree branches that waltz with the breeze. The current moves swiftly over rocks and around boulders, and, sometimes deep, sometimes shallow, reflects moving shadows and patches of light. Observing the lay of the land, I find it possible to resonate with the sheer joy my father, his siblings, and cousins felt when they scampered over the rocks, built forts, fished, and gave each other a leg up into the trees.

Though the "pipe" across the river is gone now, I can see that the distance from one side to the other would have been great enough to be daunting to the small girl that Sis was, yet to fuel her need to join the boys on the other side of the river.

I am filled with desire to enter a time when this valley was less populated, when there were no giant grocery stores, no strip malls, no traffic lights, when it was not inundated with vehicles, noise, and distraction, when children could play safely and with abandon under the watchful eyes of parents and grandparents, when every day presented adventure and discovery under the canopy of trees. If I could have been a traveler stopping by the Riverby for a night, I would have been welcomed into an extended family, enjoyed a meal prepared from a lush garden, been entertained after dinner by a band of spirited children. There would have been hours of rocking on the porch with plenty of lively conversation while the sun went down behind the mountains. I would have slept in a room with windows wide open and no sounds to keep me awake, except for the thrum of insects. Most importantly, I would have witnessed a family at work, at play, in love with life and delighted with each other.

Fortunately, I did have that kind of experience, wrapped in the warm embrace of my grandmother's Mississippi Delta home. She took all manner of tragedy in stride and somehow, probably through her faith and grace, accepted the people she loved no matter how seriously they erred or strayed.

CHAPTER TWENTY

Memory

July 4, 2009

I wanted to broach the subject with Mom yet again, but conversations in the past had turned to bitterness, anger, and mutual defenses. Why should I go through that again? Why should I subject her to painful memories? But it had been many months since we talked about the killings. During that time, something shifted. She was more open to me, eager to hear about my life. At eighty-six, she had become settled in the town where my sister lived. She had made many new friends. The last waves of her life were flowing back out into the larger mass of the ocean.

"Happy Fourth of July, Mom."

"Same to you," she said in a fresh-out-of-bed voice.

We discussed our plans for the day. She wanted to know how my daughters were getting along, how Jay was faring, the usual stuff.

"Mom, can I ask a big favor?"

With dread in her voice, she asked, "What?"

"Can we talk one more time about what happened in the Delta?" I explained to her that I was perplexed about how the incident affected her, Dad, and their relationship.

"After it happened, I was never angry with your father. I just didn't understand it."

"Did you talk to each other about it? How did Dad seem to you?"

"I really don't think he thought much about it. We never, ever, discussed the situation after he came home from the sheriff's house."

As she talked, I paced in my kitchen, a yellow legal pad nearby for notes. The smell of hot coffee tinged the air. I looked out the window at the sunlight dancing on the river's surface and reminded myself to go slowly, gently.

"How did Dad act when he was out in town, reporting, or socializing with friends?"

"If you are asking me if he showed any signs of suffering, I didn't see it. You have to remember that everyone was afraid of your grandmother. She had a lot of clout in the town and she could be very persuasive. She got your father off. If not for Beck, he wouldn't have just walked away free. It just wasn't right for him to do this and walk away. I was raised to believe that there should be consequences."

I cleared my throat and tried to swallow. Before I could press on, Mom said something that made me stand still and listen hard.

"You know, Molly, this scenario is still on my mind a lot. The cottage we stayed in had a back door that opened onto a hallway. On one side was our bedroom and on the other was the kitchen. I have a recurring nightmare that I'm in bed in that cottage and there are blacks outside waiting for your dad so they can do something to him or to me. I didn't want to lose my husband."

"Oh Mom, that's a terrifying dream. I had no idea that you were so afraid."

"I often think about what a happy life I would have had if that hadn't happened. It changed my personality. But . . . at the time I was able to cope because I had my babies, and I had some wonderful friends."

I couldn't ask her how she thought the past had changed her. She sounded vulnerable and I didn't want to take advantage of her. But I didn't really have to ask. For much of my life, I had felt the brunt of her unhappiness without the capacity to understand or have compassion or even humor. If I had known about the past, maybe I would have been a different person too.

The next few moments seemed to call for silence. Something in me was breaking apart.

"The last thing I'll say is that that night hung over me for many, many years. I wish I could have been my own self. Your father's actions and the death of my brother were in large part responsible for how my life turned out."

My heart began a slow thaw and I wanted to crawl through the telephone and put my arms around my mother. "Now I understand, Mom. You were only twenty-three and you had had more than your share of hardship. Most people never experience that much trauma in a lifetime, much less in their youth. I'm so sorry that you had to endure so much, so young."

The following three nights brought me no sleep. The picture of my mother's life filled me with sorrow. Here was a young woman newly married to a man she loved. She was full of hope for a happy family life and her baby boy embodied infinite possibilities. At that time, women were exceedingly limited in what they could make of themselves. Basically, there were only two professional careers, nursing and teaching. Upon marriage, Mom, like her peers, would have transferred her dependence from father to husband. If her chosen mate failed in some way, questions of survival would have arisen. Fears about the future filled my mother and doggedly held on throughout her life, so that she suffered from chronic anxiety and depression.

Faced with the horrors of that night in 1946, my mother made the only choice open to her. She couldn't go back to the security of her parents' home. They were still reeling from the loss of their only son. My grandfather's heart had been severely jeopardized and was failing. Mom had to make do with a marriage that was compromised from the start.

Looking back, I realize that her nervous breakdown came about as a result of her dependency on Daddy Joe. His generosity and support had continued to shore her up for many years and when he died, the pillars beneath her crumbled. Because my father was only marginally successful in his work, Mom couldn't count on him. In time, as his drinking became more problematic, he convinced my mother to support him with her inheritance.

One day, a light went on for her and she saw that if she persisted, there would be nothing left. She walked out of his life.

In the pages of this book, I have often depicted my mother in a most unkind light only because it is true to my experience of her. My desire now is to care for and about her with deep compassion for the life she has led.

May 2010

Except for a level of true understanding, only one last detail dogged me. The black Fields family members. They were the people Charles Weissinger mentioned when I first met him. At the time, I wasn't able to take that concept in, still processing other bits of information, still in denial about certain things. At last I had reached a place of acceptance—that my grandfather might have had a second family, that Simon might have been born into it. Things like this happened in those days—more often than most of us can imagine.

I sent Charles an e-mail and asked if he would meet with me so that we could talk about the black Fields family members. He agreed and told me he knew a lady, eighty years old, who looked just like my uncle Bill. While I packed to fly to Mississippi, I had the distinct feeling that I was about to meet someone who would at last illuminate the dark corners of the story.

Charles and I talked briefly in his office about the land. He made a few phone calls and arranged a late afternoon visit with Mary Shelby's grandmother, Fannie Ivory. Then we drove to the Sharkey County Courthouse so that he could show me on the map the parcels my grandfather gave to Simon's family. Charles knew all of the workers in the courthouse so well that he could tease them and make them laugh. Clearly, he was respected and admired. He flipped through the massive volumes of deed records with agility and expertise, chasing down the ownership history of each parcel. After about an hour, he settled on a family name that he believed to have been associated with the land transfer to Simon's family. I recognized the name from the title searcher's findings, and when I researched it online, I found that it belonged to a white family. Charles reshelved the volumes and prepared to go back to his office. When he reached the door of the courthouse, he turned to me and said, "There. Now you got the dirt." Such irony—"the dirt" was only a handful of loamy soil placed in my hand by Charles himself. Yes, it was a story passed down through his family, but despite my best efforts, I would not be able to verify his version of what happened or why.

Mary Shelby met me at the Rolling Fork Library and I followed her to a retirement community where her grandmother lived. Miss Ivory was not eighty years old. She was ninety-six. Born five years before Simon and seven years before my grandfather married Mamaw, she fit right into the time period when Thomas was a bachelor.

Fannie was tall and lean and fully cogent about her life, although she wanted to tell me stories that bordered on the occult. As a young woman, she'd had visions, premonitions, and warnings of imminent danger from people in her community. She told me that someone tried to poison her when she was a young teenager. She lost her sight for one day. The result of these strange experiences was that her faith had grown stronger and that was why, she believed, she was given such a long life.

But Fannie's connection with my family was negligible. She knew both of her parents' names. Her mother died when she was three years old, and her father ran away at that time, so her grandmother raised her.

"Did you know my grandfather, Thomas Fields?"

She replied, "He was a good man but you just don't bother him. Don't stir him up or you'll get a whoopin.'" Those were the first and only negative words I ever heard about him.

Fannie was light-skinned as Charles had said but she bore no resemblance to Uncle Bill.

July 2011

Nonfiction writers, like me, know that their primary role is to tell the truth, to present the facts, to steer wide and clear of conjecture and supposition, to write with clarity and transparency.

The secret my family has kept for over sixty years is now a frag-
mented, unreliable collection of memories. That function of the
mind called memory is subject to numerous imperfections. It can
distort the truth, misappropriate facts, block or omit important
details. It is subject to bias, to diminution over time, to inappropriate attribution. When I revisit the varied accounts of the
December 12, 1946, shootings, I find that the one put forth by my
father's sister, Frances Lee, offers a suggestion of what happened
that bears close scrutiny. She said that she knew who instigated
the incident but she did not intend to divulge that information
because it would "disillusion" me and my cousins. The knowledge
she refused to impart has now been interred with her. She died in
October 2010. Whoever set the events in motion could not have
anticipated the ways in which he or she would alter the lives of
those involved.

For me to put forth another version of the story requires me to
indulge in the kind of fallacious suppositioning that undermines
our memories of true events. But since this "quilting" together of
disparate parts is painful, there may be some merit in doing it.

What if:

On that December night, at the end of a frustrating harvest
when black farmers and pickers had chosen to spend their time
in the tavern, rather than in the cotton fields; when guests from
Kentucky were arriving any minute at Greenfields and Jo, whose
help with serving the meals and keeping house was desperately
needed, had departed unannounced to go in search of a man or
a bottle; when one of the black gin workers had gone joyriding in
the company car; when Sis was due to be picked up at the train
station in Leland—there was only one person in the family with
the power and might to say to Dad, Tom, and Bill, "Go to the Pan
Am station and do whatever you have to to get Jo home, and find
the car." What if it had been Mamaw who had heard that Simon,
now thirty-five, just home from serving five years in the war, had
designs on "his" land. What if the situation was that the boys had
returned home from the juke jive in a heat, sweating, angry, and

even scared; that Tom had had to be helped into the back bedroom; that Dr. Goodman had had to be phoned up and begged
to come to the house late at night; that Dad had had to wait for
Sheriff Crawford to arrive and arrest him.

What if Mamaw had met the sheriff at the door, falling to her
knees and begging him not to put Dad in jail, offering to not only
pay bail but add a little something to it for him if he would do
all in his power to stack the deck in Dad's favor. What if Dad,
realizing that the fact of two dead men would look like overt violence, instead told his mother it was self-defense, thus releasing
her from some of the blame; that way he could be exonerated, he
could tell his new wife a half or quarter truth so that she wouldn't
despise his mother any more than she already did, so that her
parents would have reason to encourage her to stay put with
their baby grandson. What if, in the middle of all of this Mamaw
had to send Bill to Leland because she couldn't go; if Bill told Sis
he wasn't anywhere near the Pan Am station that night; if upon
reaching home, Sis found Mamaw in her bed, face covered with a
black cloth. And saddest of all, what if Mamaw had taken to her
bed knowing that even though Tom would be okay, that she was
responsible for his injury, for the death of two black men, for my
father's and Bill's involvement.

And what if the story was never spoken of after that night
for one simple reason: no one in the family, especially my father,
wanted Mamaw to suffer public humiliation, loss of control, of
status and power, of her great spirit.

The errand she sent her sons to perform may have spun out of
control. There was reason to think that it might. The Pan Am had
a bad reputation for violence. I believe Mamaw suffered mightily
whether or not she had a hand in the devastation that occurred.

If I had enough evidence to accept this as true, it would not
diminish my love for Rebekah Fields, nor would it disillusion
me; it would enlarge and inform my view of her as a loving,
flawed human being as capable of making terrible mistakes as
the rest of us.

❧

I grieve for the lives of Simon and David and for their families
who still, sixty years later, mourn the loss of those young men.
I grieve for my mother and for my father. Our collective sorrow
could have been avoided were it not for the prevailing historical
and social context in which horrendous deeds were enacted with
impunity. If my beloved family and I can bear to look unflinch-
ingly at our history and tell ourselves the truth and if we can allow
ourselves to own our past and our human failings, there is hope
for forgiveness, even reconciliation.

Acknowledgments

Had I known when I started writing *Death in the Delta* that it would require so much of me, it is doubtful that I would have had the strength of will or the confidence to see my way to the last page. Providence stepped in and provided me with an extraordinarily gifted doula. I am deeply grateful to Diana Hume George, without whose keen skills as an editor this book would not have evolved into a work that I believe in and that I am proud to have written.

Craig Gill, editor-in-chief at the University Press of Mississippi, shepherded me through years of reader reviews and subsequent revisions. His steady and persistent faith in the value of this story nurtured my quest and persistence.

I would be remiss if I failed to recognize the guidance and support offered to me by the fine mentors I studied under in the Goucher College MFA Program, Suzannah Lessard, Joseph Mackall, Philip Gerard, and Thomas French. I am also indebted to the Riverbend Writers group: Sebastian Matthews, Glenda Elkins, and Janet Hurley. Special thanks to Peggy Millin, an extraordinary writing coach.

Encouragement from the Literature and Language Department at UNC–Asheville, especially Dr. Dee James, has been important in keeping me focused and invested.

Early on, I sought guidance from Joya Wesley and Jill Williams at the Greensboro Truth and Reconciliation Commission and from Deanna Mayer and Lisa Davis, writers. Essential and invaluable spiritual counseling came from Martina Glasscock Barnes, the Very Reverend Todd Donatelli and Reverend Canon Brian Cole from the Cathedral of All Souls, Reverend Jim Abbott from St. Matthias, and retired Reverend Bill Turner and his wife, Barbara.

The dedicated and ardent members of the Commission to Dismantle Racism of the Episcopal Diocese of Western North

Carolina fueled my desire to write this story with respect for all parties involved.

My deepest thank-you goes to the following Mississippians who walked beside me: Inez Files, Rose Cooper, and Emma Harris; Mr. King Evans and family, especially Carolyn Hackett; Pat Thrasher, Ray Mosby, Charles Weissinger, Merlin Richardson, Mrs. B. B. Rogers, Hugh and Mary Dayle McCormick, Trudy Schultz, Mrs. Doe, Carabelle Johnson, Mary Shelby, and Fannie Ivory; and the librarians at the Rolling Fork Library.

The following large-hearted friends talked me through the rough spots and kept me moving forward: Lean Carroll, Lynn Kessler, Candy and Boo Worrell.

And finally I thank my family, especially Jay Fields, Laura Wolf, Tommy Fields, Grover Greer, and Thomas Jarvis Greer, family genealogist. To Betsy Hall and H. J. Fields, I owe my most heartfelt gratitude, for you brought me into this "dangerous and beautiful" world and you taught me the hard lessons as well as the skills I needed to learn them.

A Note on Sources

To do justice to the subject I investigated in this book, I had to inform my thinking about a particular time in American history and a particular location. I also had to look deeply at the work of other writers who have tackled the issue of black/white relations. The following books broadened and enhanced my perspective:

Backroads of My Memory: A Collection of Memories Written over the Past Eight Years by King Evans

Blood Done Signed My Name by Tim Tyson

A Delta Diary: Amanda Worthington's Civil War Diary by Troy Woods

Healing Wounded History: Reconciling Peoples and Restoring Places by Russ Parker

Inheriting the Trade: A Northern Family Confronts Its Legacy as the Largest Slave-trading Dynasty in U.S. History by Thomas Norman DeWolf

Lanterns on the Levee: Recollections of a Planter's Son by William Alexander Percy

Mind of the South by W. J. Cash

The Most Southern Place on Earth: The Mississippi Delta and the Roots of Regional Identity by James C. Cobb

One Drop: My Father's Hidden Life: A Story of Race and Family Secrets by Bliss Broyard

Only a Few Bones: A True Account of the Rolling Fork Tragedy and Its Aftermath by John Philip Colletta

Passed On: African American Mourning Stories by Karla Holloway

Seven Sins of Memory: Insights from Psychology and Cognitive Neuroscience by Daniel L. Schacter

Slaves in the Family by Edward Ball

Southern Legacy by Hodding Carter

This Delta, This Land: An Environmental History of the Yazoo–Mississippi Floodplain by Mikko Saikku